THE PATRIOT'S
CHURCHILL

THE PATRIOT'S
CHURCHILL

AN INSPIRING COLLECTION
OF CHURCHILL'S FINEST WORDS

Richard M. Langworth, Editor

EBURY
PRESS

1 3 5 7 9 10 8 6 4 2

First published in 2011 by Ebury Press, an imprint of Ebury Publishing
A Random House Group company

The Random House Group Limited Reg. No. 954009

Addresses for companies within the Random House Group can be found
at www.randomhouse.co.uk

A CIP catalogue record for this book is available from the British Library

The Random House Group Limited supports The Forest Stewardship
Council (FSC), the leading international forest certification organisation.
All our titles that are printed on Greenpeace approved FSC certified paper
carry the FSC logo. Our paper procurement policy can be found at
www.rbooks.co.uk/environment

Mixed Sources
Product group from well-managed
forests and other controlled sources
www.fsc.org Cert no. TT-COC-2139
© 1996 Forest Stewardship Council

Designed and set by seagulls.net

Printed in the UK by CPI Mackays, Chatham, ME5 8TD

ISBN 9780091920036

To buy books by your favourite authors and register for offers visit
www.rbooks.co.uk

*To the British and
Commonwealth Armed Forces,
and to the memory of
Winston S. Churchill, 1940-2010.*

CONTENTS

INTRODUCTION

Churchill on Patriotism

Demonstrating how far our language has deteriorated, a recent thesaurus offers for 'patriot' the synonyms 'nationalist, loyalist, chauvinist, jingoist' and 'flag-waver'. The dictionary, as yet untainted, defines 'patriot' as 'a person who vigorously supports their country and is prepared to defend it against enemies or detractors'. The dictionary certainly trumps the thesaurus in Churchill's case.

In an age of widespread cynicism toward politics, *The Patriot's Churchill* reminds us that in Sir Winston's view, things can be different – by emphasising his precepts of collegiality and friendship toward political opponents, magnanimity in victory and wry reflection after defeat.

The danger in culling patriotic utterances from Churchill's 15 million published words is that they may suggest a skewed view of his broader attitudes. Churchill's fervent praise of Neville Chamberlain in the Great Britons chapter should not detract from his many earnest criticisms of Chamberlain over appeasement in the 1930s.

Churchill's words, and 35 million more words about him by colleagues, biographers and friends, is the material that informs this book, digitally scanned by Karl-George Schon, and latterly by Wayne Brent and Alfred Alvarez of Zuma Corporation in Culver City, California. My son Ian, a software engineer, created the proprietary search engine in the domain http://wsc.langworth.com, which enables me to track phrases, the vast majority from Churchill's works. No item is included unless it can be attributed, nor republished without the permission of his Literary Estate.

The arrangement of quotations is chronological where the subject is narrowly defined, as in the Freedoms chapters. In the broader chapters – such as Britain and the Commonwealth, Equality, Great Britons, Service, War and Work, Opportunity, Invention, it was found more convenient to group quotes under subheadings.

Quotations carrying a date only are from Churchill's speeches in the House of Commons: the Parliamentary Debates (Hansard). All other quotes are specifically referenced with key words, which are identified in the bibliography. For example, OB refers to the Official Biography, *Winston S. Churchill,* by Randolph S. Churchill and Sir Martin Gilbert, its biographic and companion or document volumes. (See bibliography.)

The date cited is the earliest attributable to the quotation. I have sometimes indicated the date of the quotation *and* the date it was later published, especially concerning the two world wars. Venues other than London, Chartwell or Downing Street are supplied if available. Quotes from broadcasts are identified and sources noted.

THANKS

Paul H. Courtenay, senior editor of *Finest Hour* and an indispensible proofreader and Churchill expert, who helped review my quotation book, *Churchill by Himself*, again lent his scholarship by reviewing my reviewing my manuscript. *Churchill by Himself* is also reviewed entry by entry against original sources for its second edition, and several corrections also pertain to this book, so my thanks are due the student reviewers: Catherine Helle of the University of Alaska, Anchorage, James Wegmann and Ben Hayter of Hillsdale College in Michigan, and Craig Kreinbihl of the Hillsdale faculty.

Sir Martin Gilbert, Churchill's great biographer, not only gave permission to quote from his works, but has been of inestimable encouragement to me in all my efforts, and my debt to him is great.

Paul Courtenay, senior editor of *Finest Hour* and proofreader extraordinaire, read every entry and made many suggestions and corrections which saved me from myself.

To the aforementioned Karl-George Schon, Wayne Brent, Alfred Alvarez and Ian Langworth, along with my wife Barbara (with me every step of the way), my gratitude is enormous. The late

Winston S. Churchill authorised the use of his grandfather's copyright, and Gordon Wise at Curtis Brown Group Ltd found the best publishers possible in Ebury Press. The people at Ebury, Andrew Good-fellow and Ali Nightingale, deserve an advance thanks, for most of my work is now done and theirs is just beginning.

Several Churchill Centre members have helped and inspired entries, including Randy Barber, David Boler, Paul Courtenay, Marcus Frost, General Colin L. Powell, Ambassador Paul H. Robinson and Suzanne Sigman. Ralph Keyes, editor-author of *The Quote Verifier*, helped me to get into my bones the essence and language of a good book of quotations. Fred Shapiro, editor of *The Yale Book of Quotations*, also offered sound judgement and advice.

Lastly I thank Sir Winston Leonard Spencer Churchill, K.G., O.M., P.C., etc. Where would we all be without him?

I am most anxious to hear from readers who wish to offer comments, corrections, praise or blame, to which end I refer readers to the Reviews section of my website http://richardlangworth.com, where any follow-up notes will be published.

ONE
THE FLAG

Churchill was not a flag-waver, but his romantic soul was stirred on great occasions by the flag, and he was often moved to tears. We can imagine him adding to his catalogue of 'What I Saw and Heard in America' the tendency among Americans to display the flag on poles, porches, parks and buildings. One can scarcely imagine what he would think of the mindset of some in Britain who regard the display of the Union Flag as the act of an eccentric or worse. Perhaps he would just sadly shake his head.

———————

Liberation, 1900

The gates were flung open, and while the rest of the guards – they numbered fifty-two in all – stood uncertain what to do, the long-penned-up officers surrounded them and seized their weapons. Someone – Grimshaw of the Dublin Fusiliers – produced a Union Jack (made during imprisonment out of a Vierkleur). The Transvaal emblem was torn down, and, amid wild cheers, the first British flag was hoisted over Pretoria.

1900. (HAMILTON'S, 355.)

Churchill had returned to Pretoria to take part in the liberation of his former fellow prisoners. The Vierkleur (four colours) was the flag of Transvaal.

Queen Victoria

So the Queen is dead. The news reached us at Winnipeg and this city far away among the snows – fourteen hundred miles from any British town of importance – began to hang its head and hoist half-masted flags.

1901, 22 JANUARY, WINNIPEG, MANITOBA. (OB, CV1/ 2, 1231.)

WSC to his mother. The Queen referred to was Alexandrina Victoria (1819-1901), Queen of the United Kingdom of Great Britain and Ireland, 1837-1901, Empress of India, 1876-1901).

The flag at sea

Do not overlook what naval supremacy means. It does not mean merely the command of the Channel, or of the Mediterranean, or of the Atlantic or of the Persian Gulf – it means something much wider than that – it means the power to send our ships wherever the waters roll, to fly our flag on every sea, to land our troops on any shore.

1903, 13 FEBRUARY, WALLSEND. (MBA, 80.)

Armistice Day, 1918

It was a few minutes before the eleventh hour of the eleventh day of the eleventh month ... And then suddenly the first stroke of the chime. I looked again at the broad street beneath me. It was deserted. From the portals of one of the large hotels absorbed by Government Departments darted the slight figure of a girl clerk, distractedly gesticulating while another stroke of Big Ben resounded. Then from all sides men and women came scurrying into the street. Streams of people poured out of all the buildings. The bells of London began to clash ... Flags appeared as if by magic.

1927. (CRISIS III, PART 2, 541-4.)

First World War

Here we stir the embers of the past and light the beacons of the future. Old flags are raised anew; the passions of vanished generations awake; beneath the shell-torn soil of the twentieth century the bones of long dead warriors and victims are exposed, and the wail of lost causes sounds in the wind.

1929. (CRISIS IV, 202.)

A charge to youth

Raise the glorious flags again, advance them upon the new enemies, who constantly gather upon the front of the human army, and have only to be

3

assaulted to be overthrown. Don't take No for an
answer. Never submit to failure.

1930. (MEL, 74.)

Youthful reflections

I entrenched myself around the slogan "No
slavery under the Union Jack". Slavery they
suggested might be right or wrong: the Union Jack
was no doubt a respectable piece of bunting: but
what was the moral connection between the two? I
had the same difficulty in discovering a foundation
for the assertions I so confidently made, as I have
found in arguing with the people who contend that
the sun is only a figment of our imagination.

1930. (MEL, 216.)

Second World War

The bomb had fallen in Peckham. It was a very big
one – probably a landmine. It had completely
destroyed or gutted twenty or thirty small three-
storey houses and cleared a considerable open space in
this very poor district. Already little pathetic Union
Jacks had been stuck up amid the ruins.

1940. (WW2 II, 308.)

The debt which the British Empire and Commonwealth of Nations owe to the United States for the
fact that their operations against the Japanese

shielded Australia and New Zealand from Japanese aggression and from mortal peril during a period when the Mother Country was at full stretch in the struggle against Germany and Italy, that, that is one that will never be forgotten in any land where the Union Jack is flown.

1944, 26 MARCH, BROADCAST. (DAWN, 41-2.)

In a world of confusion and ruin, the old flag flies.

1944, 21 APRIL.

Upon Britain fell the proud but awful responsibility of keeping the Flag of Freedom flying in the Old World till the forces of the New World could arrive.

1945, 16 NOVEMBER, BRUSSELS. (SINEWS, 42.)

With a gasp of astonishment and relief the smaller neutrals and the subjugated states saw that the stars still shone in the sky. Hope, and within it passion, burned anew in the hearts of hundreds of millions of men. The good cause would triumph. Right would not be trampled down. The flag of Freedom, which in this fateful hour was the Union Jack, would still fly in all the winds that blew.

1949. (WW2 II, 556.)

…none who took part in it [divine service with Roosevelt and Churchill aboard HMS *Prince of Wales*, August 1941] will forget the spectacle presented that sunlit morning on the crowded quarterdeck – the symbolism of the Union Jack and the Stars and Stripes draped side by side on the pulpit ... the close-packed ranks of British and American sailors, completely intermingled, sharing the same books and joining fervently together in the prayers and hymns familiar to both. I chose the hymns myself, "For Those in Peril on the Sea" and "Onward, Christian Soldiers". We ended with "O God, Our Help in Ages Past" ... It was a great hour to live.

1950. (WW2 III, 384.)

We fought alone against tyranny for a whole year, not purely from national motives. It is true that our lives depended upon our doing so, but we fought the better because we felt with conviction that it was not only our own cause but a world cause for which the Union Flag was kept flying in 1940 and 1941.

1950, 27 JUNE.

Cinque Ports Flag, 1946

Grace Hamblin: Mr. Churchill, Cinque Ports flag has arrived and Allen has put it up.

WSC: Callooh! Callay! Oh frabjous day! And so he chortled in his joy.

1946, CHARTWELL. (HAMBLIN, 'CHARTWELL MEMORIES'; PROCEEDINGS, 1987.)

When WSC reopened Chartwell after the war he wanted to fly his flag of Lord Warden of the Cinque Ports. Grace Hamblin (secretary, 1932-1965) said he responded in this way because he knew she was fond of Lewis Carroll's Through the Looking Glass. *(The actual words are: "O frabjous day! Callooh! Callay! / He chortled in his joy.")*

Rallying to the flag, 1957

To call into life and action the depressed and languid spirit of England; to weld all her resources of wealth and manhood into a single instrument of war which should be felt from the Danube to the Mississippi; to humble the house of Bourbon, to make the Union Jack supreme in every ocean, to conquer, to command, and never to count the cost, whether in blood or gold – this was the spirit of Pitt.

1957. (HESP III, 150.)

WSC occasionally wrote Union Jack, but technically it is a jack only when flown on the bow of a ship.

TWO
THE ISLAND RACE

Churchill believed that parliamentary government under a sovereign who reigned but did not rule was the most perfect form of democracy. He preferred the unwritten British constitution to the written American one, however much he admired the latter's wording, and wondered privately if the U.S. system of recurrent elections wasn't a detriment to waging war.

Churchill considered Britain's Crown, Parliament and Commonwealth a 'golden circle', unique in the world. Although he saw and sought to mend the rents in British society, he regarded his country with all its faults as the prime example of civilisation.

It is legitimate to consider whether Churchill's clarion calls of British pride, sentiment and instinct still apply in today's Britain. 'But what is the purpose which has brought us all together?' he asked. 'It is the conviction that the life of Britain, her glories and message to the world, can only be achieved by national unity, and national unity can only be preserved upon a cause which is larger than the nation itself.' Does this still apply? The reader may judge.

Yes, he was an old-fashioned Victorian who yearned for Britain's Antonine Age. But if British hearts, on reading these words, are not imbued however temporarily with a renewed love of country, they are stony hearts indeed.

Achievement

Little Englander as I suppose I shall be called, I have seen enough in peace and war of its frontiers and dominion to know that it could not stand for a year on a purely material foundation. The life and strength of our authority springs from moral and not from physical forces. Liberty and justice, English honesty, and English tolerance have raised the character of our homely island life above the stand-ard of neighbouring nations...

1903, 11 NOVEMBER, BIRMINGHAM TOWN HALL. (FFT, 43.)

If we in this small island have gradually grown to a considerable estate, and have been able to give our wage-earners some relief from the harder forms of economic pressure, and to build up a decent, toler-ant, compassionate, flexible, and infinitely varied society, it is because in all the great crises of our history, the interest of Britain has marched with the progress and freedom of mankind.

1939, 20 APRIL, CANADA CLUB, LONDON. (BLOOD, 152-3.)

With all our shortcomings, conditions in this country were a model to Europe and to many parts of the United States.

1943, 17 APRIL. (WW2 IV, 847.)

The wisdom of our ancestors has led us to an envied and enviable situation. We have the strongest Parliament in the world. We have the oldest, the most famous, the most honoured, the most secure, and the most serviceable, monarchy in the world. King and Parliament both rest safely and solidly upon the will of the people expressed by free and fair election on the basis of universal suffrage.

1945, 15 MAY.

These forty-six millions differ from every other community that has ever existed in the world by the fact that they are perched upon the completely artificial foundation of not providing even one half of their food, and being dependent for the purchase of the bulk of their food and raw materials on persuading foreign customers to accept the wares and the services they offer. Vast, intricate, delicate, innumerable, are the methods of acquiring external wealth which the British nation has developed in recent generations, and the population has grown step by step upon the livelihood produced.

1945, 28 NOVEMBER, FRIENDS HOUSE, LONDON. (SINEWS, 52.)

Ambiguity

In England the political opinion of men and parties grows like a tree shading its trunk with its branches, shaped or twisted by the winds, rooted according to its strains, stunted by drought or maimed by storm … In our affairs as in those of Nature there are always frayed edges, borderlands, compromises, anomalies. Few lines are drawn that are not smudged. Across the ocean it is all crisp and sharp.

1931, FEBRUARY, 'PERSONAL CONTACTS', *STRAND MAGAZINE*. (THOUGHTS, 33.)

Classes

There have always been men of power and position, who have sacrificed and exerted themselves in the popular cause; and that is why there is so little class-hatred here, in spite of all the squalor and misery which we see around us.

1908, 14 MAY, KINNAIRD HALL, DUNDEE. (LIBERALISM, 201.)

Our aristocracy has largely passed from life into history; but our millionaires – the financiers, the successful pugilists and the film stars who constitute our modern galaxy and enjoy the same kind of privileges as did the outstanding figures of the 17th and 18th centuries – are all expected to lead model lives.

1933. (MARLBOROUGH I, 39.)

We have had a leisured class. It has vanished. Now we must think of the leisured masses.

1953, 27 JULY. (MORAN, 475.)

Climate

… the British people have always been superior to the British climate. They have shown themselves capable of rising above it, and certainly they have derived from it many of those strong enduring principles and ways of life which make their existence in our island home different from any other community in the world.

1948, 10 JULY, WOODFORD, ESSEX. (EUROPE, 368.)

Destiny

Undoubtedly, this new twentieth century is not in many ways so favourable to us as the nineteenth century. A new world is growing up around us, far larger than anything previously seen, and filled with giant states and competitors.

1928, 24 JULY.

It may well be that the most glorious chapters of our history are yet to be written. Indeed, the very problems and dangers that encompass us and our country ought to make Englishmen and women of this generation glad to be here at such a time. We ought to rejoice at the responsibilities with which destiny has honoured us, and be proud that we are guardians of our country in an age when her life is at stake.

1933, 24 APRIL, ROYAL SOCIETY OF ST. GEORGE, LONDON.
(COVENANT, 93.)

We rise or we fall together. Indeed, if we survive today it is because even in bygone times our ancestors so managed that in the main the special interests of Britain conformed to the general interests of the world.

1935, 24 OCTOBER.

We have sung of "the wonderful giants of old" but can any one doubt that this generation is as good and as noble as any the nation has ever produced, and that its men and women can stand against all tests? Can any one doubt that this generation is in every way capable of carrying on the traditions of the nation and handing down its love of justice and liberty and its message undiminished and unimpaired?

1940, 18 DECEMBER, HARROW SCHOOL. (UNRELENTING, 20.)

I have an invincible confidence in the genius of Britain. I believe in the instinctive wisdom of our well-tried democracy. I am sure they will speak now in ringing tones, and that their decision will vindicate the hopes of our friends in every land and will enable us to march in the vanguard of the United Nations in majestic enjoyment of our fame and power.

1945, 30 JUNE, ELECTION BROADCAST, LONDON. (VICTORY, 211.)

…it is barely ten years since we upheld on our strong, unyielding shoulders the symbols, the honour and even perhaps the life of the free world … It does indeed seem hard that the traditions and triumphs of a thousand years should be challenged by the ebb and flow of markets and commercial and financial transactions in the vast swaying world … In all history there has never been a community so large, so complex, so sure of its way of life, poised at such a dizzy eminence and on so precarious a foundation.

1952, 11 JUNE, PRESS ASSOCIATION, LONDON. (STEMMING, 299.)

England

I am a great admirer of the Scots. I am quite friendly with the Welsh, especially one of them [Lloyd George]. I must confess to some sentiment about Old Ireland, in spite of the ugly mask she tries to wear. But this is not their night. On this one night in the whole year we are allowed to use a forgotten, almost a forbidden word. We are allowed to mention the name of our own country, to speak of ourselves as "Englishmen", and we may even raise the slogan "St. George for Merrie England" … There are a few things I will venture to mention about England. They are spoken in no invidious sense. Here it would hardly occur to anyone that the banks would close their doors against their depositors. Here no one questions the fairness of the courts of law and justice. Here no one thinks of persecuting a man on account of his religion or his race. Here everyone, except the criminals, looks on the policeman as a friend and servant of the public. Here we provide for poverty and misfortune with more compassion, in spite of all our burdens, than any other country. Here we can assert the rights of the citizen against the State, or criticize the Government of the day, without failing in our duty to the Crown or in our loyalty to the King…

1933, 24 April, Royal Society of St. George, London.
(Covenant, 91-2.)

Influence

British influence is healthy and kindly, and makes for the general happiness and welfare of mankind.

1901, 13 May.

London

…when after the enemy wearied of his attack upon the capital and turned to other parts of the country, many of us in our hearts felt anxiety lest the weight of attack concentrated in those smaller organisms should prove more effective than when directed on London, which is so vast and strong that she is like a prehistoric monster into whose armoured hide showers of arrows can be shot in vain.

1941, 14 JULY, COUNTY HALL, LONDON. (UNRELENTING, 185.)

…London will never be conquered, and will never fail, and … her renown, triumphing over every ordeal, will long shine among men.

1944, 6 JULY.

London, like a great rhinoceros, a great hippopotamus, saying: "Let them do their worst. London can take it." London could take anything. My heart goes out to the Cockneys. Any visitors we may happen to have here today – and many great nations are represented here, by all those who have borne arms with us in the struggle – they echo what I say when I say "GOOD OLD LONDON!"

1945, 9 MAY, MINISTRY OF HEALTH, LONDON. (VICTORY, 129-30.)

National life

Here in this country we know that no dark designs are harboured by our Government against the peace or wellbeing of any country. There may be mistakes, there may be muddles; but no dark designs are harboured by any British Prime Minister or Foreign

Secretary. He could not live under the conditions of British Cabinet Government if it were otherwise. But foreign countries do not always attribute to us this innocence.

1933, 13 APRIL.

The new England, or the new Britain, for we have our Welsh and Scottish friends represented [a voice: "And Northern Ireland"] – and Northern Ireland which we never forget – the new Britain and the old Britain have always dwelt side by side in our land, and it is by the union and interplay of the new impulses and the great traditions both working together ... that we have contrived to build up over generations that basis of life with its rights and tolerances, its individual freedom, its collective associations, and, above all, its infinite power of self-improvement and national progress, that decent way of life which the broad masses of our people share and for which they now show themselves prepared to fight, and if need be to die.

1942, 26 MARCH, CAXTON HALL, LONDON. (END, 104.)

Origins

Our story centres in an island, not widely sundered from the Continent, and so tilted that its mountains lie all to the west and north, while south and east is a gently undulating landscape of wooded valleys, open downs, and slow rivers. It is very accessible to the invader, whether he comes in peace or war, as pirate or merchant, conqueror or missionary … A province of the Roman Empire, cut off and left to sink or swim in the great convulsion of the Dark Ages; reunited to Christendom, and almost torn away from it once more by the heathen Dane; victorious, united, but exhausted, yielding, almost without resistance, to the Norman Conqueror; submerged, it might seem, within the august framework of Catholic feudalism, was yet capable of reappearing with an individuality of its own. Neither its civilisation nor speech is quite Latin nor quite Germanic. It possesses a body of custom which, whatever its ultimate sources may be … is being welded into one Common Law. This is England in the thirteenth century, the century of Magna Carta, and of the first Parliament.

1956. HESP I, VIII–IX.

People

…the English are essentially a warlike, though not a military, people; that is to say they are always ready to fight, though not always prepared to do so.

1897, 15 OCTOBER, NOWSHERA, INDIAN FRONTIER.
(WAR CORR. 78.)

…a blunderbuss is a traditional weapon with which the British householder defends himself from those who seek to plunder him.

1901, 13 MAY.

...the British public, and the great nation which inherits this somewhat foggy island, are less likely to be grateful for benefits received than they are for evils averted.

1927, 13 APRIL.

"Tell the truth to the British people." They are a tough people, a robust people. They may be a bit offended at the moment, but if you have told them exactly what is going on, you have insured yourself against complaints and reproaches which are very unpleasant when they come home on the morrow of some disillusion.

1932, 23 NOVEMBER.

The British people are good all through. You can test them as you would put a bucket into the sea, and always find it salt. The genius of our people springs from every class and from every part of the land. You cannot tell where you will not find a wonder. The hero, the fighter, the poet, the master of science, the organiser, the artist, the engineer, the administrator or the jurist – he may spring into fame. Equal opportunity for all, under free institutions and equal laws – there is the banner for which we will do battle against all rubber-stamp bureaucracies or dictatorships.

1945, 13 JUNE, ELECTION BROADCAST, LONDON. (VICTORY, 197.)

There is no foe they will not face. There is no hardship they cannot endure. Whether the test be sharp and short or long and wearisome, they can take it. What they do not forgive is false promises and vain boastings.

1947, 4 OCTOBER, BRIGHTON. (EUROPE, 154.)

Realm

The House will observe in the Royal Proclamation the importance and significance assigned to the word "Realm". There was a time – and not so long ago – when the word "Dominion" was greatly esteemed. But now, almost instinctively and certainly spontaneously, the many states, nations and races included in the British Commonwealth and Empire, have found in the word "Realm" the expression of their sense of unity, combined in most cases with a positive allegiance to the Crown or a proud and respectful association with it.

1952, 11 FEBRUARY.

Rule Britannia

Going back a long time ... to 27 March 1936 [Mr. Baldwin] said, according to the *Daily Herald*... "We shall have to give up certain of our toys – one is 'Britannia rules the Waves'." .... As has been often pointed out, it is "Britannia rule the Waves" – an invocation, not a declaration of fact. But if the idea

"Rule Britannia" was a toy, it is certainly one for which many good men from time to time have been ready to die.

1951, 19 APRIL.

Scotland
I have myself some ties with Scotland which are to me of great significance – ties precious and lasting. First of all, I decided to be born on St. Andrew's Day – and it was to Scotland I went to find my wife, who is deeply grieved not to be here today through temporary indisposition. I commanded a Scottish battalion of the famous 21st Regiment for five months in the line in France in the last war. I sat for fifteen years as the representative of "Bonnie Dundee", and I might be sitting for it still if the matter had rested entirely with me.

1942, 12 OCTOBER, USHER HALL, EDINBURGH. (END, 237.)

Unity
But what is the purpose which has brought us all together? It is the conviction that the life of Britain, her glories and message to the world, can only be achieved by national unity, and national unity can only be preserved upon a cause which is larger than the nation itself.

1938, 9 MAY.

Wales

Môr o gân yw Cymru i gyd.
[All Wales is a sea of song.]

1951, 6 NOVEMBER.

WSC had appointed Welshman David Llewellyn as an under-secretary to the Home Office charged with Welsh affairs, announcing, "His name is quite well known throughout the Principality." A Welsh MP shouted:"Pronounce it." Churchill did – then he stunned the House with this phrase, which he had heard at an Eisteddfod (Welsh festival) thirty years before.

War

The British people have taken for themselves this motto – "Business carried on as usual during alterations on the map of Europe."

1914, 9 NOVEMBER, GUILDHALL, LONDON. (CS III, 2340.)

No demand is too novel or too sudden to be met. No need is too unexpected to be supplied. No strain is too prolonged for the patience of our people. No suffering nor peril daunts their hearts. Instead of quarrelling, giving way as we do from time to time to moods of pessimism and of irritation, we ought to be thankful that if such trials and dangers were destined for our country we are here to share them, and to see them slowly and surely overcome.

1918, 25 APRIL, MINISTRY OF MUNITIONS, LONDON. (CS III, 2610.)

When the British people make up their minds to go to war they expect to receive terrible injuries. That is why we tried to remain at peace as long as possible.

1940, 5 SEPTEMBER.

They are the only people who like to be told how bad things are, who like to be told the worst…

1941, 10 JUNE.

The British people do not, as is sometimes thought, go to war for calculation, but for sentiment.

1945, 2 APRIL. (WW2 VI, 431.)
WSC to Marshal Stalin; one of their last communications.

THREE

COMMONWEALTH OF NATIONS

Churchill is known for his famous declaration that he had not become the King's first minister to preside over the Empire's liquidation. In fact, he saw the end coming quite early, and by the 1950s was resigned to it, not without a proud nostalgia. To those who came after him goes the credit, or the blame, for what the Commonwealth is today. But when Churchill spoke of the British Empire 'opening up the jungles' and 'mitigating poverty', he meant exactly what he said.

The years 1815 to 1914 mark Britain's 'Imperial Century.' Thanks to increased life expectancy, a precipitous decline in infant mortality, and the lack of a major imperial rival after the Napoleonic wars, a tiny island had the surplus manpower to expand an empire by 400 million people and ten million square miles. Britain provided the administrative and business climate in the West Indies, India, Canada,

Australia, New Zealand and the Pacific which survives today. In Africa the Empire was less successful, but the achievement was unmatched by any other colonial power.

Churchill believed firmly that the Empire had been a boon to the native peoples within it, and mourned its decline with a nostalgia born of certitude that the Empire had been a 'beneficent' force. He feared a premature handover from 'disinterested control of British officials to the mere self-interest of some small local community'.

Achievements and reflections

The British Empire is held together by moral not by material forces. It has grown up in liberty and silence. It is not preserved by restriction and vulgar brag. The greatest triumphs of our race have been won not for Britain only, but for mankind. When we suppressed the slave trade we were fighting in the cause of humanity ... Look where you will, you will see at every stage on the long and dangerous path on which we have moved, from the condition of a small poor island people to the enjoyment and responsibility of world-wide dominion, it has been written in letters of shining gold: "The victory of Britain means the welfare of the world."

1904, 19 FEBRUARY, FREE TRADE HALL, MANCHESTER.
(FFT, 72-3.)

It is a sober fact that the British Empire produces within its limits every commodity which luxury can imagine or industry require.

1905, 8 MARCH.

The shores of History are strewn with the wrecks of Empires. They perished because they were found unworthy. We would court – and deserve – the same fate if, in the coming years, we so denied our destiny and our duty. The problem of the empty lands is one which we cannot evade. Our answer must be Population and Development.

1938, 22 MAY, 'PEOPLING THE WIDE, OPEN SPACES OF EMPIRE', NEWS OF THE WORLD. (ESSAYS IV, 444.)

If the British Empire is fated to pass from life into history, we must hope it will not be by the slow process of dispersion and decay, but in some supreme exertion for freedom, for right and for truth.

1939, 20 APRIL, CANADA CLUB, LONDON. (BLOOD, 153-4.)

It is the duty of us all … to try our best to make this new expression of the unity of the worldwide association of states and nations [British Commonwealth] a practical and lasting success, and that is the course which we on this side of the House intend to steer.

1949, 28 APRIL.

African Empire

...the chronic bloodshed which stains the West African seasons is odious and disquieting. Moreover the whole enterprise is liable to be represented by persons unacquainted with Imperial technology as the murdering of natives and the stealing of lands.

1906, JANUARY. (HYAM, 208.)

All forms of cruelty to natives are to be reprobated, but there is one form of cruelty which is especially odious; it is when it takes the form of the exploitation of natives for the purpose of gain.

1906, 28 FEBRUARY.

I have some knowledge of the native populations in these regions and certainly we are to regard them as the greatest trust that is confided to us, because they are the most helpless of the population, and it is for us to see that they are better, and not worse, from our responsible charge of the country.

1921, 14 JULY.

Australia

The armies [in Gallipoli] are like men fighting on a high and narrow scaffold above the surface of the earth ... to step back means not merely defeat, but destruction. That is why I have always in speaking of this dwelt upon the immense importance of every yard of ground, of every furlong that is gained by the heroic courage of our soldiers and of our superb Australian fellow citizens.

1915, 17 SEPTEMBER, ENFIELD LOCK. (CS III, 2387.)

Australian and New Zealand troops may well be in contact with the enemy today. There, to the classic scenes of the ancient lands of Greece, they will bring the valour of the sons of the Southern Cross.

1941, 12 APRIL, BRISTOL UNIVERSITY. (CS, 6377.)

A young nation, like Australia, dwelling in a continent growing ample food for itself and for export, may try experiments in Socialism without the risk of fatal injury, but the fifty million gathered together in this small island are in a very different position.

1950, 21 JANUARY, PARTY BROADCAST. (BALANCE, 157.)

The heart of the country, over a million square miles, has attracted delvers after metals and ranchers of cattle, but it remains largely uninhabited. The silence of the bush and the loneliness of the desert are only disturbed by the passing of some transcontinental express, the whirr of a boomerang, or the drone of a pilotless missile.

1958. (HESP IV, 122.)

Canada

The French Canadians derived greater pleasure from singing "God Save the King" than from singing "Rule Britannia".

1904, 19 JULY.

The difficulties are to appreciate the immense size of this country which goes on for thousands of miles of good fertile land, well watered, well wooded, unlimited in possibilities. How silly for people to live crowded up in particular parts of the Empire when there is so much larger and better a life open here for millions. Half the effort of the war would have solved all these problems. However, the world is known to be unteachable.

1919, 12 AUGUST. (OB CV5/2, 45-6.)

WSC to his wife, during a railway trip to Quebec.

Darling I am greatly attracted to this country. Immense developments are going forward. There are fortunes to be made in many directions. The tide is flowing strongly. I have made up my mind that if Neville Chamberlain is made leader of the Conservative Party or anyone else of that kind, I clear out of politics and see if I cannot make you and the kittens a little more comfortable before I die. Only one goal still attracts me, and if that were barred I should quit the dreary field for pastures new. As Daniel Peggotty says, "There's mighty lands beyond the seas." However the time to take decision is not yet.

1929, 27 AUGUST, BANFF SPRINGS HOTEL, ALBERTA.
(OB CV5/2, 61-2.)

The nearest Churchill came to becoming a Canadian rancher! Daniel Peggotty was the Yarmouth fisherman, brother of David Copperfield's nurse, in Dickens's David Copperfield *(1850). The goal that still attracted Churchill was the premiership.*

Canada is a potent magnet, drawing together those in the new world and in the old whose fortunes are now united in a deadly struggle for life and honour against the common foe. The contribution of Canada to the Imperial war effort, in troops, in ships, in aircraft, in food and in finance, has been magnificent.

1941, 30 DECEMBER, CANADIAN PARLIAMENT, OTTAWA.
(UNRELENTING, 363.)

There are no limits to the majestic future which lies before the mighty expanse of Canada with its virile, aspiring, cultured and generous-hearted people. Canada is the vital link in the English-speaking world and joins across the Atlantic Ocean the vast American democracy of the United States with our famous old island and the fifty millions who keep the flag flying here.

1951, 19 NOVEMBER, GUILDHALL, LONDON. (STEMMING, 193.)

Gibraltar

The establishment of the apes on Gibraltar should be twenty-four and every effort should be made to reach this number as soon as possible and maintain it thereafter.

1944, 1 SEPTEMBER. (WW2 VI, 607.)

WSC to Colonial Secretary. Legend has it that if the apes ever leave Gibraltar Britain's rule there will end. From Churchill's time the ape colony has thrived.

India

…we wonder whether the traveller shall some day inspect, with unconcerned composure, the few scraps of stone and iron which may indicate the British occupation of India … Yet, perhaps, if that unborn critic of remote posterity would remember that "in the days of the old British" the rice crop had been more abundant, the number of acres under cultivation greater, the population larger, and the death rate lower, than at any time in the history of India – we should not be without a monument more glorious than the pyramids.

1898. (MALAKAND, 95-6.)

…on what does our rule in India depend? It is not on terror, it is not on physical force, it is not on the superior knowledge of our Government. I say that 30,000 civilians and 70,000 soldiers would be utterly insufficient to preserve our rule in India for a month if it were not known that our motives were pure and lofty, and that we sought the welfare of the Indian people. British justice is the foundation-stone of British dominion. Destroy that, and the whole stately and stupendous edifice which the glories and sacrifices of ten generations have upreared will come clattering to the ground.

1904, 19 FEBRUARY, FREE TRADE HALL, MANCHESTER. (FFT, 71.)

…the departure of the British from India, which Mr. Gandhi advocates, and which Mr. Nehru demands, would be followed first by a struggle in the North and thereafter by a reconquest of the South by the North and of the Hindus by the Moslems. This danger has not escaped the crafty foresight of the Brahmins … now that there is spread throughout India the belief that we are a broken, bankrupt, played-out power, and that our rule is going to pass away and be transferred in the name of the majority to the Brahmin sect, all sorts of greedy appetites have been excited and many itching fingers are stretching and scratching at the vast pillage of a derelict Empire.

1931, 18 MARCH, ROYAL ALBERT HALL, LONDON. (INDIA, 128, 130.)

I do not care whether you are more or less loyal to Great Britain. I do not mind about education, but give the masses more butter … Tell Mr. Gandhi to use the powers that are offered and make the thing a success … I am genuinely sympathetic towards

India. I have got real fears about the future … But you have got the things now; make a success and if you do I will advocate your getting much more.

1935. (OB V, 618-19.)

Churchill to G.D. Birla, Gandhi's friend, who lunched at Chartwell. Birla repeated the remark to Gandhi, who said, "I have got a good recollection of Mr. Churchill when he was in the Colonial Office and somehow or other since then I have held the opinion that I can always rely on his sympathy and goodwill." While this does not completely represent the WSC–Gandhi relationship, it goes a long way toward destroying the myths about it.

Malta

For now nearly two years Malta has stood against the enemy. What a thorn it has been in their side! What toll it has taken of their convoys! Can we wonder that a most strenuous effort has been made by Germany and Italy to rid themselves of this fierce aggressive foe.

1942, 23 APRIL.

New Zealand

In the first few months of the last war … nearly 2,000,000 actually demanded of their own free will to be sent overseas to the bloody trenches in France and Flanders. In far-off New Zealand nearly one-tenth of the entire population of the country traversed voluntarily more than half the globe in order to fight and die in a cause upon which they had never been consulted beforehand. Nothing like the voluntary effort of the British Empire was seen in any other country or has ever been paralleled in history.

9 JUNE 1938. (STEP, 240.)

...New Zealand troops may well be in contact with the enemy today. There, to the classic scenes of the ancient lands of Greece, they will bring the valour of the sons of the Southern Cross.

1941, 12 APRIL, BRISTOL UNIVERSITY. (CS VI, 6377.)

I was deeply touched by the telegram which you so kindly sent me on behalf of yourself and the Government and people of New Zealand. Throughout this long struggle New Zealand has never failed us, and her steadfastness and loyalty have helped to sustain us all during the darkest days. Now that victory over all our enemies is with God's help assured, I am confident that the ties which bind us so closely will grow even stronger, and that our unity of purpose will ensure a just and permanent peace.

1944, 11 JUNE. (DAWN, 124.)

Telegram to Mr. Peter Fraser, Prime Minister of New Zealand, in reply to his congratulations on the successful launching of the Normandy invasion on 6 June 1944.

Responsibility

Not since the days of the Roman Empire has a single nation carried so great a responsibility for the lives of men and women born outside her shores as Great Britain does today. Within her forty or so dependent territories dwell eighty million people for whose welfare and enlightenment Britain is, to a greater or less degree, answerable.

1960. (INGRAMS, VII.)

South Africa

Was it not rather a sad thing that Johannesburg, the great spring of wealth, where all the gold rose to the surface of the ground and where they ought to be able to pay the best wages and offer the most attractive conditions, should be in the mind of the South African native a place of melancholy tribulation and hard work?

1904, 5 MAY.

Churchill had advanced ideas on the plight of natives in South Africa. See also next chapter.

...the Government [should] take steps to improve the lot of the Chinese labourer. It would in future prevent fines, collective punishments and criminal penalties being imposed for noncriminal offences.... "undercut cruelty" by subsidising repatriation ... The spectacle of the Chinaman wandering over the veldt, his hand against every man and every man's

hand against him, with half the world between him
and his home in China, is as degrading, hideous, and
pathetic as any this civilised and Christian nation has
made itself responsible for in modern years.

1906, 15 AUGUST.

No responsible statesman, and no British Cabinet,
so far as I know, ever contemplated any other solu-
tion of the South African problem but that of full
self government ... If our policy should end in
mocking disaster, then the resulting evil would not
be confined to South Africa ... if the near future
should unfold to our eyes a tranquil, prosperous,
consolidated Afrikander nation under the protecting
aegis of the British Crown, then the good also will
not be confined to South Africa; then the cause of
the poor and the weak all over the world will have
been sustained; and everywhere small peoples will
get more room to breathe, and everywhere great
empires will be encouraged by our example to step
forward – and it only needs a step – into the
sunshine of a more gentle and more generous age...

1906, 17 DECEMBER.

Uganda

The Nile springs out of the Victoria Nyanza, a vast
body of water nearly as wide as the Thames at Westminster Bridge, and this imposing river rushes down
a stairway of rock from fifteen to twenty feet deep,

in smooth, swirling slopes of green water. It would be perfectly easy to harness the whole river and let the Nile begin its long and beneficent journey to the sea by leaping through a turbine. It is possible that nowhere else in the world could so enormous a mass of water be held up by so little masonry.

1908. (MAJ, 74-5.)

WSC referred to what was then called Ripon Falls, a watercourse submerged when building the nearby Owen Falls Dam (now the Nalubaale Power Station). In 1954 the Queen inaugurated the Owen Falls scheme and sent a message to Churchill: "Your vision has become reality" (OB II, 235).

FOUR

EQUALITY

Churchill was raised amid the prejudices of his time, and it would be silly to whitewash his views. It would be equally wrong to commit what American author William Manchester referred to as 'generational chauvinism' – judging the attitudes of a century ago by the standards of today.

For a Victorian, Churchill held remarkably enlightened views toward South African natives in 1900, Indians in South Africa in 1908, female suffrage after 1910. During the Second World War he grumpily acquiesced with allowing the U.S. Army to enforce segregation of its black soldiers; in British forces, black soldiers were integrated.

He believed generally that all people were created equal, but that colonisation by "the dominant race" was noble, provided that race took responsibility for raising up native populations – paternalism typical of the liberals in his era. At home, he supported a state-guaranteed minimum standard, above which citizens should be free to pursue their own interests, according to their lights and talents.

The impression he leaves is of a politician occupying the middle ground, but not a moderate, for he had firm opinions. He relied upon the British democracy to ensure equality and a decent life for all. He was a patrician, but not a snob; he enjoyed luxuries, but believed in taxing them; though he found fault with democracy, he always respected the little man. Justice and equality were prominent among his principles.

Importance of equality

...the only safe rule for doing justice between man and man was to assume – a large assumption in some cases – that all men are equal and that all discriminations between them are unhealthy and undemocratic.

1906, 31 JULY.

The whole foundation of our political system is the equality of rights and the equal importance and value of the political rights enjoyed by persons in every class.

1911, 30 MAY.

I have regarded compulsion not as the gathering together of men as if they were heaps of shingle, but the fitting of them into their places like the pieces in the pattern of a mosaic. The great principle of equality of sacrifice requires in practice to be applied in accordance with the maxim, "A place for every man and every man in his place".

1916, 23 MAY.

[My] hatred of Bolshevism and Bolsheviks is not founded on their silly system of economics, or their absurd doctrine of an impossible equality. It arises from the bloody and devastating terrorism which they practise in every land into which they have broken, and by which alone their criminal regime can be maintained.

1920, 8 JULY.

Let [Socialists] abandon the utter fallacy, the grotesque, erroneous, fatal blunder of believing that by limiting the enterprise of man, by riveting the shackles of a false equality ... they will increase the wellbeing of the world.

1926, 21 JANUARY. (CS IV, 3821.)

When we read about Germany, when we watch with surprise and distress the tumultuous insurgence of ferocity and war spirit, the pitiless ill-treatment of minorities, the denial of the moral protection of civilised society to large numbers of individuals solely on the ground of race ... one cannot help feeling glad that the fierce passions that are raging in

Germany have not found, as yet, any other outlet but upon Germans.

1933, 23 MARCH.

… I have always been in favour of extending the franchise. I believe in the will of the people. I do not believe in the perversion of the will of the people by actively organised and engineered minorities, who, having seized upon power by force or fraud or chicane, come forward and then use that power in the name of vast masses with whom they have long lost all effective connection.

1946, 12 DECEMBER.

We must not allow British troops or British officers in the Indian Army to become the agencies and instruments of enforcing caste Hindu domination upon the 90 million Muslims and the 60 million Untouchables; nor must the prestige or authority of the British power in India, even in its sunset, be used in partisanship on either side of these profound and awful cleavages.

1946, 12 DECEMBER.

Homosexuals
…homosexuals might indeed be a security risk, not so much because they might be subject to blackmail, but because they often feel themselves alien and

apart from the mainstream of the country, like a black in a white country, or a white in a black one.

CIRCA 1950s. (MONTAGUE BROWNE, 219-20.)

Churchill had several close homosexual friends, and his only concern about them seems clear in this remark. Yet in 2007 a shallow thinker, discovering a 1942 letter to the King in which WSC advised against a knighthood "just now" for Noël Coward, announced that this proved WSC was a homophobe.

Race

Boer commando: Well, is it right that a dirty Kaffir should walk on the pavement – without a pass too? That's what they do in your British Colonies. Brother! Equal! Ugh! Free! Not a bit. We know how to treat Kaffirs.

WSC: Probing at random I had touched a very sensitive nerve … What is the true and original root of Dutch aversion to British rule? … It is the abiding fear and hatred of the movement that seeks to place the native on a level with the white man. British government is associated in the Boer farmer's mind with violent social revolution. Black is to be proclaimed the same as white. The servant is to be raised against the master; the Kaffir is to be declared the brother of the European, to be constituted his legal equal, to be armed with political rights. The dominant race is to be deprived of their superiority; nor is a tigress robbed of her cubs more furious than is the Boer at this prospect.

1899, PRETORIA. (LADYSMITH, 131-2; BOER, 60.)

A remarkable insight to Churchill's early views on race. Though he retained the paternalistic instincts, his comments in his Boer War books raised eyebrows at the turn of the last century, when few entertained such ideas.

It must be self-evident to every one who had studied the South Africa question that the loyal cooperation of the Boers in the settlement of South Africa would be such a dazzling bribe, such an enormous advantage, that it would be inconceivable that any government acquainted with the conditions should refuse to make any considerable sacrifices to secure so desirable an end.

1902, 21 JANUARY.

Racial peace reigns throughout the islands [Bahamas] and the colour question appears completely solved. At a dinner given to me by both branches of the Legislature, considerably more than half the members – all in immaculate evening dress – were of ebon hue.

1932, 23 MARCH, 'MY HAPPY DAYS IN THE "WET" BAHAMAS', *EVENING STANDARD*. (ESSAYS IV, 98.)

Problems will arise if many coloured people settle here. Are we to saddle ourselves with colour problems

in the UK? Attracted by Welfare State. Public opinion in UK won't tolerate it once it gets beyond
certain limits. [But we should let] public opinion
develop a little more before taking action.

1954, 3 FEBRUARY (BROOK DIARIES,
SUNDAY TELEGRAPH, 5 AUGUST 2007).

I read with great interest all that you have written
me about what is called Colonialism … In this I
must admit I am a laggard. I am a bit sceptical about
universal suffrage for the Hottentots even if refined
by proportional representation. The British and
American Democracies were slowly and painfully
forged and even they are not perfect yet.

1954, 8 AUGUST. BOYLE, EISENHOWER, 167.

Women

…the Mahommedan religion increases, instead of
lessening, the fury of intolerance. It was originally
propagated by the sword, and ever since its votaries
have been subject, above the people of all other
creeds, to this form of madness. In a moment the
fruits of patient toil, the prospects of material prosperity, the fear of death itself, are flung aside.

1898. (MALAKAND, 26-7.)

The fact that in Mohammedan law every woman
must belong to some man as his absolute property –

44

either as a child, a wife, or a concubine – must delay the final extinction of slavery until the faith of Islam has ceased to be a great power among men.

1899. (RIVER II, 249.)

It may seem strange that a great advance in the position of women in the world in industry, in controls of all kinds, should be made in time of war and not in time of peace. One would have thought that in the days of peace the progress of women to an ever larger share in the life and work and guidance of the community would have grown, and that, under the violence of war, it would be cast back. The reverse is true. War is the teacher, a hard, stern, efficient teacher. War has taught us to make these vast strides forward towards a far more complete equalisation of the parts to be played by men and women in society.

1943, 29 SEPTEMBER, ROYAL ALBERT HALL, LONDON.
(ONWARDS, 224.)

I didn't like the idea of their entering Parliament but it turned out better than I feared … Concede the theory and you have no trouble in practice … You can use women in AA [anti-aircraft] batteries: why not in foreign service … Anything in law to prevent a woman becoming a judge?

1945, 19 MARCH. (BROOK DIARIES, *NEW YORK TIMES*,
22 JANUARY 2006.)

[The future role of women should be] the same, I trust, as it has been since the days of Adam and Eve.

1952, 17 JANUARY, PRESS CONFERENCE, WASHINGTON.
(FISHMAN, 394.)

Churchill had begun to favour universal female suffrage in the 1920s, as his daughter Mary remarked, "…when he realised how many women would vote for him".

When I think what women did in the war I feel sure they deserve to be treated equally.

1958. (COLVILLE, CHURCHILLIANS, 123.)

WSC was referring to the new Churchill College Cambridge, which was intended to be co-educational. John Colville wrote: 'No college at Oxford or Cambridge had ever done any such thing. I asked him afterwards if this had been Clementine's idea. "Yes," he replied, "and I support it."'

FIVE

FREEDOM
OF SPEECH

Franklin Roosevelt's 'Four Freedoms' were agreeable to Churchill; he had fought for freedom of want and fear in his own early career in Parliament. Freedom of speech seems so intrinsic to modern democracies that we tend to take it for granted. But Churchill, observing the successive rise of Bolshevism in Russia, Fascism in Italy and Nazism in Germany, knew how easily this basic right could be perverted by an entrenched dictatorship.

The Communist theme aims at universal standardisation. The individual becomes a function: the community is alone of interest: mass thoughts dictated and propagated by the rulers are the only thoughts deemed respectable ... The Beehive? No, for there must be no queen and no honey, or at least no honey for others.

1931, MAY, 'MASS EFFECTS IN MODERN LIFE', *STRAND MAGAZINE*.
(THOUGHTS, 185.)

A state of society where men may not speak their minds, where children denounce their parents to the police, where a business man or small shopkeeper ruins his competitor by telling tales about his private opinions … cannot long endure if brought into contact with the healthy outside world.

1938, 16 OCTOBER, BROADCAST TO AMERICA, LONDON. (BLOOD, 89.)

…civilisation implies, in any society, the freedom to criticise the government of the day; free speech; free press; free thought; free religious observance; no racial persecution; fair treatment of minorities; and courts of law and justice which have an authority independent of the executive and untainted by Party bias.

1939, 19 MAY.

It is in this fear of criticism that the Nazi and Bolshevik dictatorships run their greatest risk. They silence all criticism by the concentration camp, the rubber truncheon, or the firing party. Thus the men at the top must very often only be fed with the facts which are palatable to them. Scandals, corruption and shortcomings are not exposed, because there are no independent voices.

1940, 27 JANUARY, FREE TRADE HALL, MANCHESTER. (CS VI, 6189.)

The question arises, "What is freedom?" There are one or two quite simple, practical tests … namely:

Is there the right to free expression of opinion and of opposition and criticism of the Government of the day?

1944, 28 AUGUST.

The full quotation is the theme of Chapter 13. It is not incidental that, of his several tests of freedom, Churchill ranged freedom of speech first.

No Socialist Government conducting the entire life and industry of the country could afford to allow free, sharp, or violently worded expressions of public discontent. They would have to fall back on some form of Gestapo, no doubt very humanely directed in the first instance. And this would nip opinion in the bud ... it would gather all the power to the supreme party and the party leaders, rising like stately pinnacles above their vast bureaucracies of civil servants, no longer servants and no longer civil.

1945, 4 JUNE, BROADCAST, LONDON. (VICTORY, 189.)

The 'Gestapo' remark in his election campaign speech is alleged to have cost Churchill votes in the 1945 election, but Labour's landslide victory had been in part ensured by events of the previous decade.

The people of any country have the right, and should have the power by constitutional action, by free unfettered elections, with secret ballot, to choose or change the character or form of government under which they dwell: that freedom of speech and thought should reign; that courts of justice, independent of the executive, unbiased by any party, should administer laws which have received the broad assent of large majorities or are consecrated by time and custom. Here are the title-deeds of freedom which should lie in every cottage home. Here is the message of the British and American peoples to mankind.

1946, 5 MARCH, WESTMINSTER COLLEGE, FULTON, MISSOURI. (SINEWS, 97.)

One cannot say that the man or the woman in the street can be brought up violently and called to account because of expressing some opinion on something or other which is *sub judice*. They are perfectly entitled to do that. They may say things that are deplorable – many deplorable things are said under free speech.

1951, 18 JUNE.

SIX

FREEDOM OF RELIGION

Churchill was not a religious man. He encountered religious diversity early, being brought up as 'High Church', but with a nanny 'who enjoyed a very Low Church form of piety'. As a young officer in India, he read all the popular challenges to orthodox religion, like Darwin's *Origin of Species* and Wynwood-Reade's *The Martyrdom of Man*, evolving into an optimistic agnostic. He spoke jocularly of the Almighty, suggesting that he himself had made so many deposits in the 'Bank of Observance' as a boy that he had been 'drawing confidently upon it ever since', but that his Final Judgement would be 'in accordance with the principles of English Common Law'.

Churchill believed profoundly in religious freedom, and everywhere resisted persecuting Jews, Buddhists, Muslims or others from practising their beliefs. When he spoke fervently of 'Christian civilisation' he was speaking in the broader sense, to

principles he saw as universal: the Ten Command-
ments, the Sermon on the Mount, the Golden Rule,
charity, forgiveness, courage in adversity.

Times change. If a president or prime minister
went round discussing 'Christian civilisation' today,
a thousand voices would proclaim his excommuni-
cation from the Church of the Politically Correct.
Churchill would be mystified by this, as indeed
would the Jews, Buddhists and Muslims of his time
who wholeheartedly endorsed what he said about
the Second World War, which they fought together.

The conflict between good and evil which proceeds
unceasingly in the breast of man nowhere reaches
such an intensity as in the Jewish race … We owe to
the Jews in the Christian revelation a system of ethics
which, even if it were entirely separated from the
supernatural, would be incomparably the most
precious possession of mankind, worth in fact the
fruits of all other wisdom and learning put together.
On that system and by that faith there has been built
out of the wreck of the Roman Empire the whole of
our existing civilisation.

1920, 8 FEBRUARY, 'ZIONISM VS. BOLSHEVISM',
ILLUSTRATED SUNDAY HERALD. (ESSAYS IV, 26.)

First there are the Jews who, dwelling in every country throughout the world, identify themselves with
that country, enter into its national life, and, while

adhering faithfully to their own religion, regard themselves as citizens in the fullest sense of the State which has received them. Such a Jew living in England would say, "I am an Englishman practising the Jewish faith." This is a worthy conception, and useful in the highest degree.

IBID., 27.

...the State cannot control the Church in spiritual matters; it can only divorce it.

1928, 14 JUNE.

There are a few things I will venture to mention about England ... Here no one thinks of persecuting a man on account of his religion or his race.

1933, 24 APRIL, ROYAL SOCIETY OF ST. GEORGE, LONDON. (COVENANT, 91.)

I was the host and I said that if it was his [King Abdul Aziz ibn Saud, 1876-1953] religion that made him say such things, my religion prescribed as an absolute sacred ritual smoking cigars and drinking alcohol before, after, and if need be during, all meals and the intervals between them. Complete surrender.

1945, 17 FEBRUARY, LAKE FAYYUM, EGYPT. (GILBERT, LIFE, 825.)

I recollect well at the end of the last war, more than a quarter of a century ago, that the House ... did not feel inclined for debate or business, but desired to offer thanks to Almighty God, to the Great Power which seems to shape and design the fortunes of nations and the destiny of man; and I therefore beg, Sir, with your permission to move: "That this House do now attend at the Church of St. Margaret, Westminster, to give humble and reverent thanks to Almighty God for our deliverance from the threat of German domination." This is the identical Motion which was moved in former times.

1945, 8 MAY. (VICTORY, 128.)

Why is your chief [Hitler] so violent about the Jews? I can quite understand being angry with Jews who have done wrong or are against the country, and I understand resisting them if they try to monopolise power in any walk of life; but what is the sense of being against a man simply because of his birth? How can any man help how he is born?

1948. (WW2 I, 65.)

WSC in 1932, to Ernst 'Putzi' Hanfstaengl, Hitler's press aide, who later broke with Hitler and fled Germany for his life.

The flame of Christian ethics is still our highest guide. To guard and cherish it is our first interest, both spiritually and materially. The fulfilment of spiritual duty in our daily life is vital to our survival. Only by bringing it into perfect application can we hope to solve for ourselves the problems of this world and not of this world alone.

1949, 31 MARCH, MASSACHUSETTS INSTITUTE OF TECHNOLOGY, BOSTON. (BALANCE, 48.)

In the end death came as a friend; and after a happy day of sunshine and sport, and after 'good night' to those who loved him best, he fell asleep as every man or woman who strives to fear God and nothing else in the world may hope to do.

1952, 7 FEBRUARY, BROADCAST ON THE DEATH OF KING GEORGE VI, LONDON. (STEMMING, 238.)

Christ's story was unequalled and his death to save sinners unsurpassed; moreover the Sermon on the Mount was the last word in ethics.

CIRCA 1953. (COLVILLE, CHURCHILLIANS, 157.)

SEVEN

FREEDOM FROM WANT

Was Churchill's ardent support of capitalism and free enterprise contrary to his role in constructing the Welfare State? No. Dr. Larry Arnn, President of Hillsdale College in Michigan, once chief of research for Churchill's official biographer, explains: 'Churchill entered Parliament under a prime minister who opposed the principle of consent of the governed. He broke with that leader – it is striking how strongly he did so. Yet, because of Britain's rigid class system, he identified socialism as the worst domestic danger.

'Churchill was for some way of healing or bridging class distinctions and providing security for the working class, so that they would not expropriate the wealth of the holders of capital; so they would have a fair chance for themselves ... He saw the problem of bureaucracy, and of excess by the majority, very clearly from an early day. The problem is more mature now than it was in his time. That is why it is easy for some of Churchill's solutions to look leftish from our modern vantage point.

'Churchill understood that the first division in politics is between the few rich and the many poor … He was profoundly for a just society, in which the economy is driven by private enterprise, and in which money is allowed to "fructify in the pockets of people".

'If a disaffected majority, necessarily made up of the many who are poor, or relatively poor, expropriate the wealth of the few, that will destroy justice in the state, even if the poor have a grievance against the rich. Churchill was trying to prevent that. For Churchill, this is a very rich subject, rather like the writings of James Madison in America.'

We want to draw a line below which we will not allow persons to live and labour, yet above which they may compete with all the strength of their manhood. We want to have free competition upwards; we decline to allow free competition to run downwards.

1906, 11 OCTOBER, ST. ANDREW'S HALL, GLASGOW.
(LIBERALISM, 164.)

I look forward to the universal establishment of minimum standards of life and labour, and their progressive elevation as the increasing energies of production may permit. I do not think that Liberalism in any circumstances can cut itself off from this fertile field of social effort, and I would recommend you not to be scared in discussing any of these proposals, just because some old woman comes along and tells you they are Socialistic.

IBID., 164

If I had to sum up the immediate future of democratic politics in a single word I should say "insurance." That is the future – insurance against dangers from abroad, insurance against dangers scarcely less grave and much more near and constant which threaten us here at home in our own island.

1909, 23 MAY, FREE TRADE HALL, MANCHESTER. (LIBERALISM, 265.)

Everyone knows that he has a prospect of getting five shillings a week when he reaches that age. It is not much, unless you have not got it.

1911, 25 MAY.

When I think of the fate of poor old women, so many of whom have no one to look after them and nothing to live on at the end of their lives, I am glad to have had a hand in all that structure of pensions and insurance which no other country can rival and which is especially a help to them.

1930. (MEL, 87.)

I have been prominently connected with all these schemes of national compulsory organised thrift from the time when I brought my friend Sir William Beveridge into the public service thirty-five years ago, when I was creating the labour exchanges, on which he was a great authority, and when, with Sir Hubert Llewellyn Smith, I framed the first unemployment insurance scheme. The prime parent of all national insurance schemes is Mr. Lloyd George. I was his lieutenant in those distant days, and afterwards it fell to me as Chancellor of the Exchequer eighteen years ago to lower the pensions age to sixty-five and to bring in the widows and orphans.

1943, 21 MARCH, BROADCAST, LONDON. (ONWARDS, 38-9.)

Establish a basic standard of life and labour and provide the necessary basic foods for all. Once that is done, set the people free, get out of the way, and let them all make the best of themselves, and win whatever prizes they can for their families and for their country ... Only in this way will an active, independent, property-owning democracy be established.

1947, 28 OCTOBER.

All the boastings of the welfare State have to be set against the fact that more than what they have given with one hand has been filched back by the other.

1951, 21 JULY, WOODFORD, ESSEX. (STEMMING, 94.)

EIGHT

FREEDOM FROM FEAR

Churchill devoted most of his life to winning, or at least striving for, freedom from fear, the last of Franklin Roosevelt's 'Four Freedoms'. Churchill strove for it by urging preparedness, by contrasting free life in Britain with that faced by other peoples quite nearby, by demolishing unnecessary 'fear-thought', and by preaching courage. Although fond in this context of the phrase 'cottage homes', he did not waste rhetoric on grandiose promises of freedom from fear, but on prescriptions that would attain it, and more important, retain it.

———————

It is a great mistake to suppose that thrift is caused only by fear; it springs from hope as well as from fear; where there is no hope, be sure there will be no thrift.

1908, 10 OCTOBER, DUNDEE. (PEOPLE'S, 146.)

Short of being actually conquered, there is no evil worse than submitting to wrong and violence for fear of war. Once you take the position of not being able in any circumstances to defend your rights against the aggression of some particular set of people, there is no end to the demands that will be made or to the humiliations that must be accepted.

1927, 22 JANUARY, EZE, FRANCE. (OB, CV5/1, 917-18.)

Why should we fear the air? We have as good technical knowledge as any country. There is no reason to suppose that we cannot make machines as good as any country. We have – though it may be thought conceited to say so – a particular vein of talent in air piloting which is in advance of that possessed by other countries ... That being so, I ask the Government to consider profoundly and urgently the whole position of our air defence.

1933, 14 MARCH.

The re-entry into the European circle of a Germany at peace within itself, with a heart devoid of hate, would be the most precious benefit for which we could strive, and supreme advantage which alone could liberate Europe from its peril and its fear, and I believe that the British and French democracies would go a long way in extending the hand of friendship to realise such a hope.

1935, 24 OCTOBER.

There is fear in every country, all round. Even here, in this country, with some protection from distance, there is fear … What is the fear and what is the question which arises from that fear? It is, 'How are we going to stop this war which seems to be moving towards us in so many ways?'

1936, 26 MARCH.

Worry has been defined by some nerve specialists as a 'spasm of the imagination'. The mind, it is said, seizes hold of something and simply cannot let it go. Reason, argument, threats, are useless. The grip becomes all the more convulsive. But if you could introduce some new theme, in this case the practical effect of a common purpose and of cooperation for a common end, then indeed it might be that these clenched fists would relax into open hands, that the reign of peace and freedom might begin, and that science, instead of being a shameful prisoner in the galleys of slaughter, might pour her wealth abounding into the cottage homes of every land.

1937, 14 APRIL.

Fearthought is futile worrying over what cannot be averted or will probably never happen.

1937, 15 OCTOBER, "WAR IS NOT IMMINENT,"
EVENING STANDARD. (STEP, 164.)

When I look back on the perils which have been overcome, upon the great mountain waves through which the gallant ship has driven, when I remember all that has gone wrong, and remember also all that has gone right, I feel sure we have no need to fear the tempest. Let it roar, and let it rage. We shall come through.

1941, 7 MAY.

We must confront our perils and trials with that national unity which cannot be broken, and a national force which is inexhaustible. We must confront them with resilience and ingenuity which are fearless, and above all with the inflexible will-power to endure and yet to dare for which our island race has long been renowned.

1942, 26 MARCH, CONSERVATIVE CENTRAL COUNCIL, CAXTON HALL, LONDON. (END, 108.)

Is the ordinary peasant or workman, who is earning a living by daily toil and striving to bring up a family free from the fear that some grim police organisa-tion under the control of a single party, like the Gestapo, started by the Nazi and Fascist parties, will tap him on the shoulder and pack him off without fair or open trial to bondage or ill-treatment? These simple practical tests are some of the title-deeds on which a new Italy could be founded.

1944, 28 AUGUST. (DAWN, 170.)

When asked how he would judge whether the new Ital-ian government was a true democracy. For Churchill's complete tests of freedom, see Chapter 13.

The family is gathered round the fireside to enjoy the scanty fruits of their toil and to recruit their exhausted strength by the little food that they have been able to gather. There they sit. Suddenly there is a knock at the door, and a heavily armed policeman appears. He is not, of course, one who resembles in any way those functionaries whom we honour and obey in the London streets. It may be that the father or son, or a friend sitting in the cottage, is called out and taken off into the dark, and no one knows whether he will ever come back again, or what his fate has been. All they know is that they had better not inquire. There are millions of humble homes in Europe at the moment, in Poland, in Czechoslovakia, in Austria, in Hungary, in Yugoslavia, in Rumania, in Bulgaria – where this fear is the main preoccupation of the family life.

1945, 16 AUGUST.

When we look back on all the perils through which we have passed and at the mighty foes we have laid low and all the dark and deadly designs we have frustrated, why should we fear for our future? We have come safely through the worst. 'Home is the sailor, home from the sea, And the hunter home from the hill.'

IBID.

It is a curious fact about the British Islanders, who hate drill and have not been invaded for nearly a thousand years, that as danger comes nearer and grows they become progressively less nervous; when it is imminent they are fierce; when it is mortal they are fearless. These habits have led them into some very narrow escapes.

1948. (WW2 I, 310.)

What is it that all these wage-earners, skilled artisans, soldiers, and tillers of the soil require, deserve, and may be led to demand? Is it not a fair chance to make a home, to reap the fruits of their toil, to cherish their wives, to bring up their children in a decent manner and to dwell in peace and safety, without fear or bullying or monstrous burdens or exploitations, however this may be imposed upon them? That is their heart's desire. That is what we mean to win for them.

1948, 7 May, The Hague, Netherlands. (Europe, 315.)

"It would seem," as I wrote, "that the sum of all American fears is to be multiplied by the sum of all British fears, faithfully contributed by each Service."

1951. (WW2 IV, 584.)

On differences of opinion between the American and British military leaders on how to exploit the victory in North Africa in 1942.

If the human race wishes to have a prolonged and indefinite period of material prosperity, they have only got to behave in a peaceful and helpful way towards one another, and science will do for them all that they wish and more than they can dream ... We might even find ourselves in a few years moving along a smooth causeway of peace and plenty instead of roaming around on the rim of Hell. For myself I am an optimist – it does not seem to be much use being anything else – and I cannot believe that the human race will not find its way through the problems that confront it, although they are separated by a measureless gulf from any they have known before ... Thus we may by patience, courage, and in orderly progression reach the shelter of a calmer and kindlier age.

1954, 9 OCTOBER, GUILDHALL, LONDON. (ALLIANCE, 193-5.)

NINE
FREEDOM
TO VOTE

Churchill's philosophy generally was 'one person, one vote', but as a political thinker, he entertained doubts from time to time about expanding the franchise, which went from male landowners to universal within the first fifty years of his life. During the Great Depression (see 1934 below), he experimented with the idea of a 'bonus vote', later amplified by writers like Nevil Shute; and with proportional representation, which he later rejected, while leaving it within the realm of 'theoretical principle' (see 1953 below). His position on votes for women was more nuanced than his critics allow. In 1910 (see below), he favoured suffrage for woman heads of household, but considered the Parliamentary Franchise (Women) Bill then being considered 'onesided and undemocratic'. It lost, 299-189. After

the First World War, observing women's contribution to the struggle, he came round to favouring
votes for all women 'especially,' his daughter
remarked, 'when he realised how many would vote
for him'.

———————

The principle of "one vote, one value" is in itself an
orthodox and unimpeachable principle of democracy. It is a logical, numerical principle. If the
attempt be made to discriminate between man and
man because one has more children and lives in the
country, it would be arguable that we should
discriminate because another man has more brains
or more money, or lives in the town, or for any other
of the many reasons that differentiate one human
being from another. The only safe principle, I think,
is that for electoral purposes all men are equal, and
that voting power, as far as possible, should be
evenly distributed among them.

1906, 5 APRIL.

I do not wish to be committed at the present junc-
ture to any special form or basis in or upon which
the franchise is to be granted to women. I have not
sufficiently studied the bearings of the municipal
franchise which you now favour. I am, however,
anxious to see women relieved in principle from a

disability which is injurious to them whilst it is based on grounds of sex.

1910, 19 APRIL, HOME OFFICE, WSC TO H.N. BRAILSFORD. (OB, CV2/3, 1434.)

Votes for women is so unpopular that by-elections will be unfavourable … What a ridiculous tragedy it will be if this strong Government and party which has made its mark in history were to go down on Petticoat politics! … The only safe and honest cure is to have a referendum – first to the women to know if they want it; and then to the men to know if they will give it. I am quite willing to abide by the result.

1911, 18 DECEMBER, ADMIRALTY. (OB, CV2/3, 1473.)

I propose that every householder, by which I mean the man or woman who pays the rent and the rates of any dwelling in which more than two persons habitually reside, should have a second or plural vote. This would certainly involve four or five million persons. Many of them would be young persons: a proportion of them would be women. They would all be persons who had to face the real problems of life in a manner quite different from lodgers of all kinds of both sexes, dependent or otherwise…

There is one other reform in the franchise which should be made by the present Parliament and should become operative at the next election. I mean the institution of Proportional Representation for the great cities.

The lack of influence on affairs of our great cities like Liverpool, Manchester, Glasgow, Birmingham, Bradford, Leeds and many others is deplorable. As political entities they are already moribund. They had more influence in the old days when they only had a couple of members than they have now that they are each sliced up into ten or a dozen constituencies. There is no collective voice from any of them ... On the other hand, the introduction of Proportional Representation in the counties would be a great mistake. Whereas in the cities Proportional Representation would focus the personality of the citizens, the same system in the counties would destroy the personal contacts and collective identities which exist.

1934, 14 JANUARY, 'RESTORING THE LOST GLORY OF DEMOCRACY', *EVENING STANDARD*. (ESSAYS II, 307-8.)

The part which our women played in winning the War was enshrined in the grant to them of the vote which for so many years they had vainly sought to wrest from successive Governments by methods too often suggesting that they had not the civic sense to use the privilege rightly. It was the War which solved that problem, as it solved so many others in our internal affairs.

1938, FEBRUARY, 'WOMEN IN WAR', *STRAND MAGAZINE*. (ESSAYS I, 380-86.)

Have the people the right to turn out a Government of which they disapprove, and are constitutional means provided by which they can make their will apparent?

1944, 28 AUGUST.

For the complete text of Churchill's tests of freedom, see Chapter 13.

At the bottom of all the tributes paid to democracy is the little man, walking into the little booth, with a little pencil, making a little cross on a little bit of paper – no amount of rhetoric or voluminous discussion can possibly diminish the overwhelming importance of that point.

1944, 31 OCTOBER.

King and Parliament both rest safely and solidly upon the will of the people expressed by free and fair election on the basis of universal suffrage.

1945, 15 MAY.

It is quite true that I expressed a view many years ago [see 1934 entry above], which I have seen no reason to dismiss from the region of theoretical principle, in favour of proportional representation in great cities. I have not expressed any views in favour of proportional representation as a whole, on account of the proved ill effects it has had on so many Parliaments.

1953, 17 FEBRUARY.

Proportional representation matches the percentage of a party's votes to the percentage of its seats in a legislature. While it more accurately reflects the preferences of the electorate, WSC saw it as preventing the legislative programme of the majority party and leading to a proliferation of parties and unstable coalitions.

TEN
GREAT BRITONS

'Gratitude was not the Great Man's long suit,' said the author of a recent contentious book about Churchill in a letter to me. 'He suggested that Robert Boothby be put on a bomb disposal unit.' 'What's the source?' I asked. One can always take isolated remarks made in heat or in haste or spontaneously, in unguarded private moments, and read distortions into them.

The idea that Churchill cared nothing for other people, so frequently inferred by his critics, resounds oddly to students of his words. In reviewing what Churchill said about fellow Britons, we mainly find appreciation, understanding and, in the end, magnanimity. His final view of someone usually ends on a generous note, even toward those he had severely criticised. One is hard pressed to find anything approaching hatred. Toward enemies like Hitler he was vituperative; yet even here there were traces of a stubborn willingness to try to find something worthwhile, somewhere.

These tributes to Great Britons are culled from *Churchill By Himself*. They are Churchill's heroes. I have left out those he held in less than full esteem. For these and many more, including non-Britons, the reader may refer to *Churchill By Himself*.

Alexander, Field Marshal Sir Harold

...one whose eye in military matters I have learned to trust and whose judgement of values and of difficult events has so often shone in courage and in wisdom.

1952, 1 JULY.

Harold Rupert Leofric George Alexander, Field Marshal the Hon. Sir Harold Alexander, became Earl Alexander of Tunis (1891-1969), Commander 15th Army Group in the Second World War, later the last British Governor General of Canada.

Asquith, H.H.

...if, as was inevitable in the rough and tumble of life, he was forced to submit and bow to the opinions of others, to the force of events, to the passions of the hour, it was often with barely concealed repugnance and disdain. If one is to select his greatest characteristic, this massive finality stands forth, for good or ill, above and beyond all others.

1928, AUGUST. 'HERBERT HENRY ASQUITH', PALL MALL. (GC, 89.)

H.H. Asquith, First Earl of Oxford and Asquith (1852-1928), last prime minister of a Liberal Government (1908-15).

Auchinleck, Claude

[Relieving him] was a terrible thing to have to do. He took it like a gentleman. But it was a terrible thing. It is difficult to remove a bad General at the height of a campaign: it is atrocious to remove a good General. We must use Auchinleck again. We cannot afford to lose such a man from the fighting line.

1942, 6 NOVEMBER. (NICOLSON II, 259.)

Field Marshal Sir Claude John Eyre Auchinleck (1884-1981), Commander-in-Chief Middle East (1941-42).

Baden–Powell, Robert

He was a man of character, vision and enthusiasm, and he passed these qualities on to the movement which has played, and is playing, an important part in moulding the character of our race. Sturdiness, neighbourliness, practical competence, love of country, and above all, in these times, indomitable resolve, daring, and enterprise in the face of the enemy, these are the hallmarks of a Scout...

1942, 16 JULY, BOY SCOUTS ASSOCIATION, LONDON. (END, 191.)
The First Baron Baden-Powell (1857-1941), known as B.-P., founder of the Scout Movement.

Balfour, Arthur

As I observed him regarding with calm, firm and cheerful gaze the approach of Death, I felt how foolish the Stoics were to make such a fuss about an event so natural and so indispensable to mankind. But I felt also the tragedy which robs the world of all the wisdom and treasure gathered in a great man's life and experience and hands the lamp to some impetuous and untutored stripling, or lets it fall shivered into fragments upon the ground.

1931, APRIL, 'ARTHUR JAMES BALFOUR',
STRAND MAGAZINE. (GC, 151-63.)

Arthur James Balfour, First Earl of Balfour (1848-1930), Prime Minister 1902-05.

Beatty, David

In Sir David Beatty we have a Commander-in-Chief who, by his gifts and also by his exceptional training, not only possesses the regular qualifications which admirals of distinction possess, but who has, perhaps in a greater degree than almost any of the principal officers of the fleet, what may be called the "war mind".

1917, 21 FEBRUARY.
Admiral of the Fleet David Beatty, First Earl Beatty (1871-1936).

Beaverbrook, Lord

We belonged to an older political generation. Often we had been on different sides in the crises and quarrels of those former days; sometimes we had even been fiercely opposed; yet on the whole a relationship had been maintained which was a part of the continuity of my public life, and this was cemented by warm personal friendship.

1950. (WW2 IV, 66–7.)
William Maxwell Aitken, First Baron Beaverbrook (1879-1964), Anglo-Canadian press owner and politician, WSC's first Minister of Aircraft Production. One of Churchill's oldest and dearest friends, though they did not always see eye to eye. Their relationship spanned half a century.

Bevin, Ernest

…he takes his place among the great Foreign Secretaries of our country, [and,] in his steadfast resistance to Communist aggression, in his strengthening of our ties with the United States and in his share of building up the Atlantic Pact, he has rendered services to Britain and to the cause of peace which will long be remembered.

1951, 17 MARCH, BROADCAST, LONDON. (STEMMING, 29.)

Ernest Bevin (1881–1951), Labour MP, Minister of Labour in the wartime coalition, Foreign Secretary in the post-war Labour Government.

Birkenhead, Lord (F.E. Smith)

He had all the canine virtues in a remarkable degree – courage, fidelity, vigilance, love of the chase … Some men when they die after busy, toilsome, successful lives leave a great stock of scrip and securities, of acres or factories or the goodwill of large undertakings. F.E. banked his treasure in the hearts of his friends, and they will cherish his memory till their time is come.

1936, 1 MARCH, 'BIRKENHEAD', *NEWS OF THE WORLD.*
(GC, 109, 116.)

Frederick Edwin Smith, First Earl of Birkenhead (1872-1930), known as 'F.E.', Conservative MP and lawyer, WSC's best friend.

Bracken, Brendan

Had he joined the ranks of the time-servers and careerists who were assuring the public that our air force was larger than that of Germany, I have no doubt that he would long ago have attained high office.

1940, 2 JUNE. (LYSAGHT, 177.)
Brendan Bracken, First Viscount Bracken (1901-58), newspaper owner and editor, Irish-born Conservative MP 1929-51, outspoken partisan and friend of WSC.

Brooke, Rupert

Rupert Brooke is dead ... A voice had become audible, a note had been struck, more true, more thrilling, more able to do justice to the nobility of our youth in arms engaged in this present war, than any other – more able to express their thoughts of self-surrender, and with a power to carry comfort to those who watch them so intently from afar. The voice has been swiftly stilled. Only the echoes and the memory remain; but they will linger.

1915, 26 APRIL, 'RUPERT BROOKE', *THE TIMES.* (ESSAYS III, 18.)
Rupert Chawner Brooke (1887-1915), a poet famous for his First World War sonnets, notably 'The Soldier'.

Chamberlain, Joseph

He loved the roar of the multitude, and with my father could always say, "I have never feared the English democracy." The blood mantled in his cheek, and his eye as it caught mine twinkled with pure enjoyment. I must explain that in those days we had a real political democracy led by a hierarchy of statesmen, and not a fluid mass distracted by newspapers.

1930. (MEL, 372.)

Joseph Chamberlain (1836-1914), Liberal statesman and early mentor to young Churchill, leader of Liberal Unionists, father of Austen and Neville Chamberlain.

Chamberlain, Neville

History with its flickering lamp stumbles along the trail of the past, trying to reconstruct its scenes, to revive its echoes, and kindle with pale gleams the passion of former days. What is the worth of all this? The only guide to a man is his conscience; the only shield to his memory is the rectitude and sincerity of his actions...

12 NOVEMBER 1940, TRIBUTE TO NEVILLE CHAMBERLAIN.

It fell to Neville Chamberlain in one of the supreme crises of the world to be contradicted by events, to be disappointed in his hopes, and to be deceived and cheated by a wicked man. But what were these hopes in which he was frustrated? What was that faith that was abused? They were surely among the most noble and benevolent instincts of the human heart – the love of peace, the toil for peace, the strife for peace, the pursuit of peace, even at great peril, and certainly to the utter disdain of popularity or clamour ... He was, like his father and his brother Austen before him, a famous member of the House of Commons, and we here assembled this morning, members of all parties, without a single exception, feel that we do ourselves and our country honour in saluting the memory of one whom Disraeli would have called an "English worthy."

1940, 12 NOVEMBER.

Arthur Neville Chamberlain (1869-1940), Prime Minister 1937-40.

Chaplin, Charlie

He is a marvellous comedian – bolshy in politics and delightful in conversation.

1929, 29 SEPTEMBER, BARSTOW, CALIFORNIA. (OB, CV5/2, 97.)

Charles Spencer Chaplin (1889-1977), English comedy actor and Hollywood film star.

Churchill, Jennie

She shone for me like the Evening Star. I loved her dearly – but at a distance. [In advancing my career she] cooperated energetically from her end. In my interest she left no wire unpulled, no stone unturned, no cutlet uncooked.

1930. (MEL, 19, 167.)

Lady Randolph Churchill (1854-1921), WSC's mother, was the former Jennie Jerome; she married Lord Randolph Churchill in early 1874.

Churchill, Randolph

Like Disraeli, he had to fight every mile in all his marches ... In his speeches he revealed a range of thought, an authority of manner, and a wealth of knowledge, which neither friends nor foes attempted to dispute.

1906. (LRC, XII, 145.)

Lord Randolph Churchill (1849-95), WSC's father, rose to be Chancellor of the Exchequer, but resigned over a trivial matter at the end of 1886 and did not rise again. He died aged only forty-six, most likely of a brain tumour.

Cripps, Stafford

His intellectual and moral passions were so strong that they not only inspired but not seldom dominated his actions. They were strengthened and also governed by the working of a powerful, lucid intelligence and by a deep and lively Christian faith. He strode through life with a remarkable indifference to material satisfaction or worldly advantages.

1952, 23 APRIL.

The Hon. Sir Richard Stafford Cripps (1889-1952), Labour MP, Chancellor of the Exchequer in the postwar Labour Government.

Curzon, George

His facility carried him with a bound into prolixity; his ceremonious diction wore the aspect of pomposity; his wide knowledge was accused of superficiality … [his] reverses were supported after the initial shocks with goodwill and dignity. But undoubtedly they invested the long and strenuous career with ultimate disappointment. The morning had been golden; the noontide was bronze; and the evening lead. But all were solid, and each was polished till it shone after its fashion.

1929, JANUARY. 'GEORGE CURZON'. *PALL MALL*. (GC, 174, 184.)

The Hon. George Nathaniel Curzon, First Marquess Curzon of Kedleston K.G. G.C.S.I. G.C.I.E. P.C. (1859-1925), Viceroy of India and Conservative Foreign Secretary.

Disraeli, Benjamin

He loved his country with a romantic passion. He had a profound faith in the greatness of the English character, and a burning desire to bring about an improvement in the condition of the people.

1944, 31 DECEMBER, MESSAGE TO THE PRIMROSE LEAGUE. (DAWN, 326.)

Benjamin Disraeli, First Earl of Beaconsfield (1804-81), Conservative MP, Prime Minister 1868, 1874-80.

Eden, Anthony

From midnight till dawn I lay in my bed consumed by emotions of sorrow and fear. There seemed one strong young figure standing up against long, dismal, drawling tides of drift and surrender, of wrong measurements and feeble impulses. My conduct of affairs would have been different from his in various ways, but he seemed to me at this moment to embody the life-hope of the British nation, the grand old British race that had done so much for men, and had yet some more to give. Now he was gone. I watched the daylight slowly creep in through the windows, and saw before me in mental gaze the vision of Death.

1948. (WW2 I, 201.)

Robert Anthony Eden (1897-1977), First Earl of Avon, Conservative MP and thrice Foreign Secretary between 1935 and 1955; Prime Minister, 1955–57. Eden resigned as Chamberlain's foreign minister on 20 February 1938. This is one of WSC's few admissions of doubting Britain's ability to survive.

Fisher, 'Jackie'

[The more] Lord Fisher's contribution to our naval efficiency is studied and examined, and tested by the passage of time, the more certainly will it be established that there has been within living memory no naval administrator possessed of abilities so rare and so distinguished.

1912, 5 AUGUST.

Admiral of the Fleet John Arbuthnot 'Jackie' Fisher, First Baron Fisher (1841-1920), known for reforms such as the conversion from coal- to oil-fired ships. His resignation as First Sea Lord precipitated Churchill's removal from the Admiralty in 1915, but WSC remained his admirer.

Gladstone, William

Mr. Gladstone was frequently portrayed as Julius Caesar, an august being crowned with myrtle, entitled to the greatest respect, a sort of glorified headmaster. We knew he was Prime Minister and the cleverest man in the country; a man of virtue, correctitude, and impeccability, the sort of man who was always telling you what you had done wrong, and never had to form up and be told what he had done wrong himself; the sort of man who made the rules and enforced them and never had to break them. He was venerable, majestic, formidable, benevolent.

1931, JUNE, 'CARTOONS AND CARTOONISTS', *STRAND MAGAZINE*.
(THOUGHTS, 11.)

William Ewart Gladstone (1809-98), Liberal MP, Prime Minister 1867-74, 1880-85, 1886, 1892-94.

Halifax, Edward

In Edward Halifax we have a man of light and leading, whose company is a treat and whose friendship it is an honour to enjoy. I have often disagreed with him in the twenty years I have known him in the rough and tumble of British politics, but I have always respected him and his actions because I know that courage and fidelity are the essence of his being.

1941, 9 JANUARY, LONDON, PILGRIMS SOCIETY LUNCHEON
FOR LORD HALIFAX, LONDON. (CS VI, 6328.)

Edward Frederick Lindley Wood, First Earl of Halifax, Viscount Halifax (1881-1959), Foreign Secretary at the 1938 Munich Agreement; earlier Viceroy of India; on this occasion he was Churchill's ambassador-designate to the United States.

Jellicoe, John

Jellicoe was the only man on either side who could lose the war in an afternoon.

1927. (CRISIS III, PART 1, 112.)

John Rushworth Jellicoe, First Earl Jellicoe (1859-1935), Commander-in-Chief, Grand Fleet, British commander at the inconclusive Battle of Jutland, 1916.

King George V

His reign has seen enormous perils and a triumph the like of which the annals of war cannot equal. It has seen moral, social, political and scientific changes in the life of all countries and of all classes so decisive that we, borne along upon the still hurrying torrent, cannot even attempt to measure them. The means of locomotion, the art of flying, the position of women, the map of Europe, the aims and ideals of all nations – East and West, white and black, brown and yellow – have undergone a prodigious transformation. But here at the centre and summit of the British Empire, in what is the freest society yet achieved in human record, a King who has done his duty will be reverenced by the ceremonial of his ancestors and acclaimed by the cheers of his faithful people.

1935, 9 MAY, 'THE KING'S TWENTY-FIVE YEARS',
EVENING STANDARD. (ESSAYS III, 240.)

George Frederick Ernest Albert (1865-1936), King of the United Kingdom of Great Britain and Ireland and Emperor of India, 1910-36.

King George VI

I do not think that any Prime Minister has ever received so much personal kindness and encouragement from his Sovereign as I have. Every week I have my audience, the greater part of which occurs most agreeably at luncheon, and I have seen the King at close quarters in every phase of our formidable experiences. I remember well how in the first months of this administration the King would come

in from practising with his rifle and his tommy-gun
in the garden at Buckingham Palace, and if it had
come to a last stand in London, a matter which had
to be considered at one time, I have no doubt that
His Majesty would have come very near departing
from his usual constitutional rectitude by disregard-
ing the advice of his Ministers.

1945, 15 MAY.

*Albert Frederick Arthur George (1895-1952), King
of the United Kingdom of Great Britain and Ireland
(from 1949, of Northern Ireland only) from 1936,
Emperor of India (until 1947).*

Lauder, Harry

Let me use the words of your famous minstrel – he
is here today – words which have given comfort and
renewed strength to many a burdened heart: "Keep
right on to the end of the road, Keep right on to
the end."

1942, 12 OCTOBER, USHER HALL, EDINBURGH. (END, 243.)

*Sir Harry Lauder (1870-1950), Scottish entertainer.
Music hall songs were Churchill's favourites.*

Lawrence, Thomas Edward
('Lawrence of Arabia')

He was indeed a dweller upon the mountain tops
where the air is cold, crisp and rarefied, and where

the view on clear days commands all the Kingdoms of the world and the glory of them … one of those beings whose pace of life was faster and more intense than the ordinary. Just as an aeroplane only flies by its speed and pressure against the air, so he flew best and easiest in the hurricane. He was not in complete harmony with the normal. The fury of the Great War raised the pitch of life to the Lawrence standard. The multitudes were swept forward until their pace was the same as his. In this heroic period he found himself in perfect relation both to men and events.

1935, 26 MAY, 'LAWRENCE OF ARABIA'S NAME WILL LIVE!',
NEWS OF THE WORLD. (GC, 104.)

Lieutenant Colonel Thomas Edward Lawrence (1888-1935), renowned for helping to lead the Arab revolt from the Turks in the First World War; author of The Seven Pillars of Wisdom, *and exactly the kind of swashbuckling figure who appealed to WSC.*

Lloyd George, David

His warm heart was stirred by the many perils which beset the cottage homes: the health of the breadwinner, the fate of his widow, the nourishment and upbringing of his children, the meagre and haphazard provision of medical treatment and sanatoria and the lack of any organised accessible medical service from which the mass of the wage earners and the poor in those days suffered. All this excited his wrath. Pity and compassion lent their powerful wings.

1945, 28 MARCH.

David Lloyd George, First Earl Lloyd-George of Dwyfor (1863-1945), Welsh MP, Liberal Prime Minister 1916-22.

Marlborough, First Duke of

[Marlborough's] toils could only be for England, for that kind of law the English called freedom, for the Protestant religion, and always in the background for that figure, half mystic symbol and the rest cherished friend, the Queen.

1934. (MARLBOROUGH II, 260.)

John Churchill, First Duke of Marlborough (1650-1722), soldier and statesman, the subject of WSC's most masterful biography. See 'Queen Anne' below.

Montgomery, Bernard

...a Cromwellian figure, austere, severe, accomplished, tireless, his life given to the study of war, who has attracted to himself in an extraordinary measure the confidence and the devotion of his Army.

1943, 11 FEBRUARY.

Field Marshal Bernard Law Montgomery, First Viscount Montgomery of Alamein (1887-1976), known as 'Monty'.

Morley, John
Such men are not found today. Certainly they are not found in British politics. The tidal wave of democracy and the volcanic explosion of the War have swept the shores bare ... The old world of culture and quality ... was doomed; but it did not lack its standard-bearer.

1929, NOVEMBER. 'JOHN MORLEY', *PALL MALL*; (GC, 61-5).
John Morley, First Viscount Morley of Blackburn (1838–1923), Liberal MP, writer and editor.

Queen Anne
On her throne she was as tough as Marlborough in the field.

1936. (MARLBOROUGH III, 185.)
Queen Anne (1665-1714), Queen of England, Scotland and Ireland (to 1707); Queen of the United Kingdom of Great Britain and Ireland, 1707-14.

Queen Elizabeth II
Our Island no longer holds the same authority or power that it did in the days of Queen Victoria. A vast world towers up around it and after all our victories we could not claim the rank we hold were it not for the respect for our character and good sense and the general admiration not untinged by envy for our institutions and way of life. All this has

already grown stronger and more solidly founded during the opening years of the present Reign, and I regard it as the most direct mark of God's favour we have ever received in my long life that the whole structure of our new formed Commonwealth has been linked and illuminated by a sparkling presence at its summit.

1955, 18 APRIL, SICILY. (OB VIII, 1127-8.)

Elizabeth Alexandra Mary (1926-), Queen of the United Kingdom of Great Britain and Northern Ireland, 1952-.

Rosebery, Earl of

Rosebery flourished in an age of great men and small events … He was one of those men of affairs who add to the unsure prestige of a minister and the fleeting successes of an orator the more enduring achievements of literature. Some of his most polished work is found in his Rectorial Addresses and in his appreciations of great poets and writers like Burns and Stevenson.

1929, OCTOBER. 'LORD ROSEBERY', *PALL MALL.* (GC, 10, 13).

Archibald Philip Primrose, Fifth Earl of Rosebery (1847–1929), succeeded Gladstone as Liberal Prime Minister, 1894–95.

Shaw, George Bernard

...I possess a lively image of this bright, nimble, fierce, and comprehending being, Jack Frost dancing bespangled in the sunshine, which I should be very sorry to lose ... He makes his characters talk blithely about killing men for the sake of an idea; but would take great trouble not to hurt a fly ... When nations are fighting for life, when the Palace in which the Jester dwells not uncomfortably is itself assailed, and everyone from Prince to groom is fighting on the battlements, the Jester's jokes echo only through deserted halls, and his witticisms and commendations, distributed evenly between friend and foe, jar the ears of hurrying messengers, of mourning women and wounded men. The titter ill accords with the tocsin, or the motley with the bandages.

1929, AUGUST, 'BERNARD SHAW', *PALL MALL*. (GC, 27, 30, 34.)
George Bernard Shaw (1856-1950), celebrated Irish playwright, literary critic and socialist, but nevertheless a friend of WSC.

Wavell, Archibald

General Wavell, commander-in-chief of all the armies of the Middle East, has proved himself a master of war; sage, painstaking, daring, and tireless.

1941, 9 FEBRUARY, BROADCAST, LONDON. (CS VI, 6346.)
Archibald Percival Wavell (1883-1950) commanded British Forces in the Middle East, 1939-41 and British

Forces in India, 1941, 1942-43; later Viceroy and Governor General of India, 1943-47.

Wellington, Duke of

Wellington was always at his coolest in the hottest of moments.

1957. (HESP III, 374.)

Arthur Wellesley, First Duke of Wellington (1769-1852), defeated Napoleon at Waterloo; twice Prime Minister 1828-30, 1834.

ELEVEN

INDEPENDENCE

Perhaps most susceptible to charges that times have changed are Churchill's attitudes toward British independence. He spoke as the confident, or at least outwardly confident, leader of an Empire-Commonwealth, in a day when it was unimaginable that Britain might one day be anything but a first-rate power. His words have been used by soothsayers today to show that he would be both for and against the European Community, for and against the United Nations, for and against 'Coalitions of the Willing'. What more thoughtful readers of his words might pause to consider, however, is his essential faith in the just society of the British democracy – how, whatever the challenges, mechanisms were in place to weather any storm, if only the people and their leaders would avail themselves of them.

He spoke also of the independence of other countries, in words that cheered surreptitious listeners gathered around clandestine radios, and his admirers in North America. It would not be Churchill if we did not include a few examples of his words on 'independence abroad'.

Independence at Home

We used to be a source of fuel; we are increasingly becoming a sink. These supplies of foreign liquid fuel are no doubt vital to our industry, but our ever-increasing dependence upon them ought to arouse serious and timely reflection. The scientific utilisation, by liquefaction, pulverisation and other processes, of our vast and magnificent deposits of coal, constitutes a national object of prime importance.

1928, 24 APRIL.

Clearly, Churchill was considering coal–oil conversion rather in advance of most of us.

Our island is surrounded by the sea. It always has been, and although the House may not realise it, the sea was in early times a great disadvantage because an invader could come across the sea and no one knew where he would land; very often he did not know himself.

1933, 14 MARCH.

…if we wish to detach ourselves and lead a life of independence from European entanglements, we have to be strong enough to defend our neutrality.

IBID.

Not to have an adequate air force in the present state of the world is to compromise the foundations of national freedom and independence.

IBID.

Putting the preservation of peace in the first place, what is the next great object that we must have in view? … We must be independent. We must be free. We must preserve our full latitude and discretion of choice. In the past we have always had this freedom and independence.

IBID.

All history has proved the peril of being dependent upon a foreign State for home defence instead of upon one's own right arm. This is not a Party question, not a question between pacifists and militarists, but one of the essential independence of character of our island life and its preservation from intrusion or distortion of any kind.

1934, 8 MARCH.

British policy for four hundred years has been to oppose the strongest power in Europe by weaving together a combination of other countries strong enough to face the bully. Sometimes it is Spain, sometimes the French monarchy, sometimes the French Empire, sometimes Germany. I have no doubt who it is now. But if France set up to claim the overlordship of Europe, I should equally endeavour to oppose them. It is thus through the centuries we have kept our liberties and maintained our life and power.

1936, 6 MAY. (OB, CV5/3, 143.)

…we have our own dream and our own task. We are with Europe, but not of it. We are linked, but not comprised. We are interested and associated, but not absorbed. And should European statesmen address us in the words which were used of old, "Wouldest thou be spoken for to the king, or the captain of the host?," we should reply, with the Shunammite woman: "I dwell among mine own people."

1938, 9 MAY, 'THE UNITED STATES OF EUROPE',
NEWS OF THE WORLD. (ESSAYS II, 185.)

In the Bible, II Kings 4, the Shunammite woman acted out of kindness and not for personal gain.

Many people, no doubt, honestly believe that they are only giving away the interests of Czechoslovakia, whereas I fear we shall find that we have deeply compromised, and perhaps fatally endangered, the safety and even the independence of Great Britain and France.

1938, 5 OCTOBER.

Following the Munich Pact.

We are an old nation. It is nearly a thousand years since we were conquered. We have built up our state and way of life slowly and gradually, across the centuries. Therefore we can afford to make exertions for peace which would not be easy in a race less sure of itself and of its duty.

1939, 28 JUNE, CARLTON CLUB, LONDON. (BLOOD, 177-8.)

...of all races in the world our people would be the last to consent to be governed by a bureaucracy. Freedom is their life-blood.

1943, 21 MARCH, WORLD BROADCAST, LONDON. (ONWARDS, 41.)

In my country the people can do as they like, although it often happens that they don't like what they have done.

1946, 1 FEBRUARY, PRESS CONFERENCE, HAVANA, CUBA.
(GILBERT, LIFE, 864.)

Conservatives [support] a property-owning democracy. And the more widely it is distributed and the more millions there are to share in it, the more will the British democracy continue to have the spirit of individual independence, and the more they will turn their backs on the Socialist delusion that one ought to be proud of being totally dependent on the State.

1950, 14 FEBRUARY, EDINBURGH. (BALANCE, 202.)

I am honoured indeed by these experiences which I believe are unique for one who is not an American citizen. It is also of great value to me, on again becoming the head of His Majesty's Government, to come over here and take counsel with many trusted friends and comrades of former anxious days … I have not come here to ask you for money to make life more comfortable or easier for us in Britain. Our standards of life are our own business and we can only keep our self-respect and independence by looking after them ourselves.

1952, 17 JANUARY, CONGRESS, WASHINGTON. (STEMMING, 220.)

I care above all for the brotherhood of the English-speaking world, but there could be no true brotherhood without independence founded as it can only be on solvency. We do not want to live upon others and be kept by them, but faithfully and resolutely to earn our own living, without fear or favour, by the sweat of our brow, by the skill of our craftsmanship and the use of our brains.

1953, 10 OCTOBER, MARGATE. (ALLIANCE, 59.)

Independence Abroad
During the winter of 1918 and the early summer of 1919 … it is not surprising that the independence of Estonia, Latvia and Lithuania existed for the time

being only in the aspirations of their inhabitants and the sympathies of the allied and associated Powers.

1929. (CRISIS IV, 100.)

...I feel it most agreeable to recall to you that the Jeromes were rooted for many generations in American soil, and fought in Washington's armies for the independence of the American Colonies and the foundation of the United States. I expect I was on both sides then. And I must say I feel on both sides of the Atlantic Ocean now.

1941, 16 JUNE, BROADCAST TO THE UNITED STATES, LONDON.
(UNRELENTING, 165-6.)

Do not despair, brave Norwegians: your land shall be cleansed not only from the invader but from the filthy Quislings who are his tools. Be sure of yourselves, Czechs: your independence shall be restored. Poles, the heroism of your people standing up to cruel oppressors, the courage of your soldiers, sailors and airmen, shall not be forgotten: your country shall live again and resume its rightful part in the new organisation of Europe. Lift up your heads, gallant Frenchmen: not all the infamies of Darlan and of Laval shall stand between you and the restoration of your birthright. Tough, stout-hearted Dutch, Belgians, Luxemburgers, tormented, mishandled, shamefully cast-away peoples of Yugoslavia, glorious Greece, now subjected to the crowning insult of the rule of the Italian jackanapes: yield not an inch! Keep your souls clean from all contact with the Nazis; make them feel even in their fleeting hour of brutish triumph that they are the moral outcasts of mankind. Help is coming; mighty forces are arming in your behalf. Have faith. Have hope. Deliverance is sure.

1941, 24 AUGUST. (UNRELENTING, 236-7.)

TWELVE

THE
INDIVIDUAL

Churchill was an individualist. He preferred sports where individuals could shine, polo being paramount, where his 'slashing attack' made him formidable. Growing up amidst Victorian giants like his father, Gladstone, Disraeli, Salisbury, Morley and Joseph Chamberlain, he was inculcated in the 'Great Man' theory of history – that good or ill is decided not by the mass, but by individuals.

But with the 1914 Armageddon and its aftermath of dislocation, Communism, Fascism, depression and National Socialism, Churchill began to wonder thoughtfully about whether the individual still counted. In 1945 he triumphed over Fascism, but not Communism. And no sooner had victory been assured than the nation rejected him for a socialist utopia – which he fought manfully, but more weakly, than he had fought Hitler.

Toward the end, Churchill felt optimistic that the 'individual power of men and women' would continue to help his country and its kindred democracies move forward into the 'broad, sunlit uplands' he contemplated from afar in 1940. Whether that will be the case, or whether we shall yet be overcome by what he called 'Mass Effects in Modern Life', is, unfortunately, very much a lingering question.

———————

No man can be a collectivist alone ... He must be both an individualist and a collectivist ... collectively we light our streets and supply ourselves with water ... But we do not make love collectively, and the ladies do not marry us collectively, and we do not die collectively, and it is not collectively that we face the sorrows and the hopes, the winnings and the losings of this world of accident and storm.

1906, 11 OCTOBER, ST. ANDREW'S HALL, GLASGOW.
(LIBERALISM, 163.)

Trade Unions are not Socialistic. They are undoubtedly individualist organisations, more in the character of the old Guilds, and lean much more in the direction of the culture of the individual than in that of the smooth and bloodless uniformity of the mass.

1908, 14 MAY, KINNAIRD HALL, DUNDEE. (LIBERALISM, 197.)

In America opinions are taken from the standard textbooks and platforms are made by machinery according to the exigencies of party without concern for individuals. We produce few of their clear-cut political types or clear-cut party programmes. In our affairs as in those of Nature there are always frayed edges, borderlands, compromises, anomalies.

1931, FEBRUARY, 'PERSONAL CONTACTS', *STRAND MAGAZINE*.
(THOUGHTS, 32.)

Is not mankind already escaping from the control of individuals? Are not our affairs increasingly being settled by mass processes? Are not modern conditions – at any rate throughout the English-speaking communities – hostile to the development of outstanding personalities and to their influence upon events; and lastly if this be true, will it be for our greater good and glory?

1931, MAY, 'MASS EFFECTS IN MODERN LIFE', *STRAND MAGAZINE*.
(THOUGHTS, 183.)

After many miseries and prolonged confusion, there arose into the broad light of day the conception of the right of the individual; his right to be consulted in the government of his country; his right to invoke the law even against the State itself.

—1938, 16 OCTOBER, BROADCAST, LONDON. (BLOOD, 85.)

This is no war for domination or imperial aggrand-
isement or material gain; no war to shut any
country out of its sunlight and means of progress.
It is a war, viewed in its inherent quality, to establish, on impregnable rocks, the rights of the individual, and it is a war to establish and revive the
stature of man.

1939, 3 SEPTEMBER.

Peaceful Parliamentary countries, which aim at freedom for the individual and abundance for the mass,
start with a heavy handicap against a dictatorship
whose sole theme has been war, the preparation for
war, and the grinding up of everything and every-
body into its military machine.

1939, 12 NOVEMBER.

I have always taken the view that the fortunes of
mankind in its tremendous journey are principally
decided for good or ill – but mainly for good, for
the path is upward – by its greatest men and its
greatest episodes.

1941, 9 JANUARY, PILGRIMS SOCIETY LUNCHEON
FOR LORD HALIFAX, LONDON. (CS VI, 6328.)

In moving steadily and steadfastly from a class to a
national foundation in the politics and economies of
our society and civilisation, we must not forget the
glories of the past, nor how many battles we have

fought for the rights of the individual and for human freedom.

1943, 21 MARCH, BROADCAST, LONDON. (ONWARDS, 40-41.)

Will the rights of the individual, subject to his duties to the State, be maintained and asserted and exalted?

1944, 28 AUGUST. (DAWN, 170)

For Churchill's complete tests of freedom see the theme of the next chapter.

The choice is between two ways of life: between individual liberty and State domination; between concentration of ownership in the hands of the State and the extension of ownership over the widest number of individuals; between the dead hand of monopoly and the stimulus of competition; between a policy of increasing restraint and a policy of liberating energy and ingenuity; between a policy of levelling down and a policy of opportunity for all to rise upwards from a basic standard.

1949, 23 JULY, WOLVERHAMPTON. (CS VII, 7835.)

[P]lanning, with all the resources of science at its disposal, should aim at giving the individual citizen as many choices as possible of what to do in all the ups and downs of daily life ... This kind of planning differs fundamentally from the collectivist theme of grinding them all up in a vast State mill...

1949, 14 OCTOBER, EMPRESS HALL, LONDON. (BALANCE, 115.)

The power of man has grown in every sphere except over himself. Never in the field of action have events seemed so harshly to dwarf personalities. Rarely in history have brutal facts so dominated thought or has such a widespread individual virtue found so dim a collective focus. The fearful question confronts us: Have our problems got beyond our control? Undoubtedly we are passing through a phase where this may be so.

1953, 10 DECEMBER. (CS VIII, 8515.)
Speech on receiving the Nobel Prize for Literature, read by Lady Churchill in Oslo, since WSC was meeting with Eisenhower in Bermuda.

It seems to me that you [Nehru] might be able to do what no other human being could in giving India the lead, at least in the realm of thought, throughout Asia, with the freedom and dignity of the individual as the ideal rather than the Communist Party drill book.

1955, 21 FEBRUARY. (OB VIII, 1094.)
There is no saying what he would think of today's world, but it is safe to believe WSC would approve of the great democracy India has become.

[There are] complications and palliatives of human life that will render the schemes of Karl Marx more out of date and smaller in relation to world problems than they have ever been before. The natural forces are working with greater freedom and greater opportunity to fertilise and vary the thoughts and the power of individual men and women ... in the main human society will grow in many forms not comprehended by a party machine.

1957. (WW2 ABRIDGED EDITION, 973.)

THIRTEEN

LIBERTY AND FREEDOM

In his brilliant 1981 book *Churchill's Political Philosophy*, Sir Martin Gilbert puts his unerring finger on Sir Winston Churchill's core value. He does so in reporting the words of Eric Seal, Churchill's Principle Private Secretary from September 1939 until mid-1941:

> *The key word in any understanding of Winston Churchill is the simple word 'Liberty'. Throughout his life, through many changes and vicissitudes, Winston Churchill stood for liberty. He intensely disliked, and reacted violently against, all attempts to regiment and dictate opinion. In this attitude, he was consistent through his political life.*

Churchill detested – and reacted violently against – any foreign nation that threatened not only British liberty but the liberty of its neighbours. Domestically, as Paul Alkon notes in *Churchill on the Home Front* (1992), WSC resisted 'all peacetime plans for the regulation and control of the economy. They smacked to him of regimentation and dictatorship. Churchill was often dismissed as an adventurer but it was, of course, this quality of individualism for which, above all else, he stood.'

He said and wrote so much about liberty and freedom that selecting the choicest remarks is a difficult task, and readers should pursue the full speeches and books mentioned in the attributions below.

———————

The Declaration of Independence is not only an American document. It follows on Magna Carta and the Bill of Rights as the third great title-deed on which the liberties of the English-speaking people are founded. By it we lost an Empire, but by it we also preserved an Empire.

1918, 4 JULY, LIBERTY DAY MEETING, LONDON. (CS III, 2615.)

The central principle of Civilisation is the subordination of the ruling authority to the settled customs of the people and to their will as expressed through the Constitution … When civilisation reigns in any country, a wider and less harassed life is afforded to the masses of the people. The traditions of the past are cherished, and the inheritance bequeathed to us by former wise or valiant men becomes a rich estate to be enjoyed and used by all … Civilisation will not last, freedom will not survive, peace will not be kept, unless a very large majority of mankind unite together to defend them and show themselves possessed of a constabulary power before which barbaric and atavistic forces will stand in awe.

1938, 2 JULY, UNIVERSITY OF BRISTOL. (BLOOD, 53-4.)

…the cause of freedom has in it a recuperative power and virtue which can draw from misfortune new hope and new strength.

1938, 16 OCTOBER, BROADCAST, LONDON. (BLOOD, 84.)

The House of Commons … is the citadel of British liberty; it is the foundation of our laws; its traditions and privileges are as lively today as when it broke the arbitrary power of the Crown and substituted that Constitutional Monarchy under which we have enjoyed so many blessings … I do not know how else this country can be governed than by the House of Commons playing its part in all its broad freedom in British public life.

1943, 28 OCTOBER.

The question arises, "What is freedom?" There are one or two quite simple, practical tests by which it can be known in the modern world in peace conditions – namely:

Is there the right to free expression of opinion and of opposition and criticism of the Government of the day? Have the people the right to turn out a Government of which they disapprove, and are constitutional means provided by which they can make their will apparent?

Are their courts of justice free from violence by the Executive and from threats of mob violence, and free from all association with particular political Parties?

Will these courts administer open and well-established laws which are associated in the human mind with the broad principles of decency and justice?

Will there be fair play for poor as well as for rich, for private persons as well as Government officials?

Will the rights of the individual, subject to his duties to the State, be maintained and asserted and exalted?

Is the ordinary peasant or workman, who is earning a living by daily toil and striving to bring up a family free from the fear that some grim police organization under the control of a single party, like the Gestapo, started by the Nazi and Fascist parties, will tap him on the shoulder and pack him off without fair or open trial to bondage or ill-treatment?

These simple practical tests are some of the title-deeds on which a new Italy could be founded.

1944, 28 AUGUST. (DAWN, 170.)

When asked how he would judge whether the new Italian government was a true democracy.

[…we] must never cease to proclaim in fearless tones the great principles of freedom and the rights of man which are the joint inheritance of the English-speaking world and which through Magna Carta, the Bill of Rights, the Habeas Corpus, trial by jury, and the English Common Law, find their most famous expression in the American Declaration of Independence…

1946, 5 MARCH, WESTMINSTER COLLEGE, FULTON, MISSOURI. (SINEWS, 97.)

Mr. Attlee [said], "How can we clear up in six years the mess of centuries?" The mess of centuries! This is what the Prime Minister considers Britain and her Empire represented when in 1945 she emerged honoured and respected from one end of the world to the other by friend and foe alike after her most glorious victory for freedom. "The mess of centuries" – that is all we were. The remark is instructive because it reveals with painful clarity the Socialist point of view and sense of proportion. Nothing happened that was any good until they came into office. We may leave out the great struggles and achievements of the past – Magna Carta, the Bill of Rights, Parliamentary institutions, Constitutional Monarchy, the building of our Empire – all these were part of "the mess of centuries". Coming to more modern times, Gladstone and Disraeli must have been pygmies. Adam Smith, John Stuart Mill … and in our lifetime Balfour,

Asquith and Morley, all these no doubt were "small fry". But at last a giant and a Titan appeared to clear up "the mess of centuries". Alas, he cries, he has had only six years to do it in … Now the Titan wants another term of office.

1951, 12 OCTOBER, WOODFORD, ESSEX. (STEMMING, 142.)

FOURTEEN

PEACE

In a charming polemic of selective quotes, American political commentator and politician Patrick Buchanan set out to establish Churchill's 'lust' for war by quoting him on 28 July 1914: 'Everything tends towards catastrophe & collapse. I am interested, geared up and happy. Is it not horrible to be built like that?…' Of course he doesn't use the rest of this passage: '…The preparations have a hideous fascination for me. I pray to God to forgive me for such fearful moods of levity. Yet I would do my best for peace, and nothing would induce me wrongfully to strike the blow.'[1]

Such misanalysis does not give us a true picture of the man. Yes, Churchill favoured fighting wars with might and main, and entered them with gusto and even relish. More often missed were his countless efforts to prevent wars from ever happening: from placating the Boers in 1900 to a meeting of the minds with the Soviets fifty years later.

---

1. Gilbert (OB, CV II, Part 3, 1969, 1389.)

It was Churchill who proposed a Great Power 'naval holiday' to forestall the First World War, who sought 'collective security' to prevent the Second World War, who helped write an Irish Treaty that kept the peace for fifty years, who resolved the problems of Turkey's former Middle East empire, who argued on behalf of India's 'untouchables', and who championed the rights of small countries. In his closing years he was despondent – that the peace he sought was still a distant goal.

———————

Once you are so unfortunate as to be drawn into a war, no price is too great to pay for an early and victorious peace.

1901, 13 MAY.

The first indispensable condition of democratic progress must be the maintenance of European peace. War is fatal to liberalism. Liberalism is the world-wide antagonist of war.

1906, 11 OCTOBER, ST. ANDREW'S HALL, GLASGOW.
(LIBERALISM, 158.)

By a sober and modest conduct, by a skilful diplomacy, we can in part disarm and in part divide the elements of potential danger. But two things have to be considered: First, that our diplomacy depends in great part for its effectiveness upon our naval position; and that our naval strength is the one great balancing force which we can contribute to our own safety and to the peace of the world.

1914, 17 MARCH.

Over a long period of years the peace and order of the British Empire was, in fact, maintained by about seventy-five battalions abroad and seventy-five at home, with the due proportion of the other arms … To find a parallel you have to go back to the greatest period of the Roman Empire, to the age of the Antonines; to find a parallel for so great and so wide a peace being sustained upon so slender an armed force you have to go back to the Antonines, and even then the parallel is greatly in favour of the British example.

1920, 23 FEBRUARY.

The world on the verge of its catastrophe [in 1914] was very brilliant. Nations and Empires crowned with princes and potentates rose majestically on every side, lapped in the accumulated treasures of the long peace. All were fitted and fastened – it seemed securely – into an immense cantilever. The two mighty European systems faced each other glittering and clanking in their panoply, but with a tranquil gaze … The old world in its sunset was fair to see.

1923. (CRISIS I, 188.)

[Armistice Day 1918:] Is this the end? Is it to be merely a chapter in a cruel and senseless story? Will a new generation in their turn be immolated to square the black accounts of Teuton and Gaul? Will our children bleed and gasp again in devastated lands? Or will there spring from the very fires of conflict that reconciliation of the three giant combatants, which would unite their genius and secure to each in safety and freedom a share in rebuilding the glory of Europe?

1927. (CRISIS III, PART 2, 541-4.)

...those who can win a war well can rarely make a good peace, and those who could make a good peace would never have won the war. It would perhaps be pressing the argument too far to suggest that I could do both.

1930. (MEL, 346.)

I would rather have a peace-keeping hypocrisy than straightforward, brazen vice, taking the form of unlimited war.

1937, 14 APRIL.

It fell to Neville Chamberlain in one of the supreme crises of the world to be contradicted ... But what were these hopes in which he was frustrated? What was that faith that was abused? They were surely among the most noble and benevolent instincts of the human heart – the love of peace, the toil for peace, the strife for peace, the pursuit of peace, even at great peril, and certainly to the utter disdain of popularity or clamour.

1940, 12 NOVEMBER.

It is not given to us to peer into the mysteries of the future. Still, I avow my hope and faith, sure and inviolate, that in the days to come the British and American peoples will for their own safety and for the good of all walk together side by side in majesty, in justice, and in peace.

1941, 26 DECEMBER, CONGRESS OF THE UNITED STATES,
WASHINGTON. (UNRELENTING, 361.)

In years of peace, the peoples of the British Commonwealth and those of the United States are easy-going folk, wishing to lead a free life, with active politics and plentiful opportunities of innocent diversion and of national self-improvement. They do not covet anything from others, perhaps because they have enough themselves; and they have often failed to keep a good look-out upon their own safety. They have many martial qualities, but they certainly do not like drill. Nevertheless, when they are attacked and assailed and forced in defence of life and liberty to make war, and to subject all their habits of life to war conditions and to war discipline, they are not incapable ... of making the necessary transformation ... Such nations do not become exhausted by war. On the contrary, they get stronger as it goes on.

1943, 8 JUNE.

I am of opinion that if the Allies at the peace table at Versailles had not imagined that the sweeping away of long-established dynasties was a form of progress, and if they had allowed a Hohenzollern, a Wittels-bach, and a Habsburg to return to their thrones, there would have been no Hitler.

1945, 26 APRIL. (WW2 VI, 643.)

WSC to Sir Hughe Knatchbull-Hugessen, then British Ambassador in Brussels.

The [atomic] bomb brought peace, but men alone can keep that peace, and henceforward they will keep it under penalties which threaten the survival not only of civilisation but of humanity itself.

1945, 16 AUGUST.

We must make sure that its [the United Nations] work is fruitful, that it is a reality and not a sham, that it is a force for action, and not merely a froth-ing of words, that it is a true temple of peace in which the shields of many nations can some day be hung up, and not merely a cockpit in a Tower of Babel … I spoke earlier of the Temple of Peace. Workmen from all countries must build that temple.

1946, 5 MARCH, WESTMINSTER COLLEGE, FULTON, MISSOURI. (SINEWS, 95, 98.)

…the Navy has a dual function. In war it is our means of safety; in peace it sustains the prestige, repute and influence of this small island; and it is a major factor in the cohesion of the British Empire and Commonwealth. The tasks which the Navy has performed in peacetime are hardly less magnificent than those they have achieved in war. From Trafalgar onwards, for more than 100 years Britannia ruled the waves. There was a great measure of peace, the freedom of the seas was maintained, the slave trade was extirpated, the Monroe Doctrine of the United States found its sanction in British naval power ... and in those happy days the cost was about £10 million a year.

1948, 8 MARCH.

...the whole question of the Middle East might have been settled ... on the morrow of victory, and ... an Arab Confederation ... and one Jewish State might have been set up, which would have given peace and unity throughout the whole vast scene.

1948, 10 DECEMBER.

Well, there you are, you're in it [NATO] now, because there's no way out, but if we pool our luck and share our fortunes I think you will have no reason to regret it ... you have not only to convince the Soviet Government that you have superior force – that they are confronted by superior force – but that you are not restrained by any moral consideration, if the case arose, from using that force with

complete material ruthlessness. And that is the greatest chance of peace, the surest road to peace.

1949, 25 MARCH, NEW YORK, DINNER GIVEN BY HENRY LUCE.
(GILBERT, LIFE, 883-4.)

There lies before [mankind], as he wishes, a golden
age of peace and progress. All is in his hand. He has
only to conquer his last and worst enemy – himself.
With vision, faith and courage, it may be within our
power to win a crowning victory for all. Moralists
may find it a melancholy thought that peace can find
no nobler foundations than mutual terror.

1950, 28 MARCH.

Appeasement in itself may be good or bad according
to the circumstances. Appeasement from weakness
and fear is alike futile and fatal. Appeasement from
strength is magnanimous and noble and might be
the surest and perhaps the only path to world peace.

1950, 14 DECEMBER.

If I stay on for the time being bearing the burden of
my age it is not because of love for power or office.
I have had an ample share of both. If I stay it is
because I have a feeling that I may through things
that have happened have an influence on what I care
about above all else, the building of a sure and lasting peace.

1953, 10 OCTOBER, CONSERVATIVE CONFERENCE, MARGATE.
(ALLIANCE, 67.)

I still believe that vast and fearsome as the human scene has become, personal contacts of the right people in the right place at the right time may yet have a potent and valuable part to play in the cause of peace which is in our hearts.

1955, 14 MARCH.

The Middle East is one of the hardest-hearted areas in the world. It has always been fought over, and peace has only reigned when a major power has established firm influence and shown that it would maintain its will. Your friends must be supported with every vigour and if necessary they must be avenged. Force, or perhaps force and bribery, are the only things that will be respected. It is very sad, but we had all better recognise it. At present our friendship is not valued, and our enmity is not feared.

1958. (MONTAGUE BROWNE, 166-7.)

FIFTEEN
RULE OF LAW

Churchill was a believer in laws designed to foster independence of spirit, and ensure that people remain responsible for their own well-being. He certainly believed that no elected official is above the law, and reacted violently toward those whose actions suggested they thought otherwise.

Churchill believed that the judicial traditions of Britain and America and the English-Speaking Peoples, rightly understood, reflected truths of unchanging vitality and application – to all persons and all times. He thought socialism and bureaucracy – a far milder version of the latter than is currently the rule – incompatible with human liberty and even with the survival of nations. He believed that certain codes of morality find sanction in a permanent law, not made by mankind. A violation of this law is, he believed, always wrong. Virtue, not creativity, was his touchstone.

His Majesty's Government are bound by the laws which they administer. They are not above the law.

1906, 22 FEBRUARY.

Harsh laws are at times better than no laws at all.

1906, 28 FEBRUARY.

Martial law is no law at all. Martial law is brute force. Of course all martial law is illegal, and an attempt to introduce illegalities into martial law, which is not military law, is like attempting to add salt water to the sea.

1906, 2 APRIL.

…no more force should be used than is necessary to secure compliance with the law.

1920, 8 JULY.

As always happens when prohibitions are imposed which do not carry public opinion with them, there is both wholesale evasion and occasional connivance, and the law is brought into disrepute.

1926, 26 APRIL.

Here no one questions the fairness of the courts of law and justice.

1933, 24 APRIL, ROYAL SOCIETY OF ST. GEORGE, LONDON.
(COVENANT, 92.)

In this island we have today achieved in a high degree the blessings of civilisation. There is freedom; there is law; there is love of country … there is a widening prosperity. There are unmeasured opportunities of correcting abuses and making further progress.

1938, 2 JULY, UNIVERSITY OF BRISTOL. (BLOOD, 53.)

There are few words which are used more loosely than the word "Civilisation". What does it mean? It means a society based upon the opinion of civilians. It means that violence, the rule of warriors and despotic chiefs, the conditions of camps and warfare, of riot and tyranny, give place to parliaments where laws are made, and independent courts of justice in which over long periods those laws are maintained. That is Civilisation – and in its soil grow continually freedom, comfort, and culture.

IBID.

[We look] backwards to our own history, to Magna Carta, to Habeas Corpus, to the Petition of Right, to Trial by Jury, to the English Common Law and to Parliamentary democracy.

1939, 20 APRIL, CANADA CLUB, LONDON. (CS VI, 6107.)

Law, language, literature – these are considerable factors. Common conceptions of what is right and decent, a marked regard for fair play, especially to the weak and poor, a stern sentiment of impartial justice, and above all the love of personal freedom, or as Kipling put it: "Leave to live by no man's leave underneath the law" – these are common conceptions on both sides of the ocean among the English-speaking peoples.

1943, 6 SEPTEMBER, HARVARD UNIVERSITY, CAMBRIDGE, MASSACHUSETTS. (ONWARDS, 182-3.)

It must be remembered that the function of Parliament is not only to pass good laws, but to stop bad laws.

1944, 4 APRIL.

Are their courts of justice free from violence by the Executive and from threats of mob violence, and free from all association with particular political Parties? Will these courts administer open and well-established laws which are associated in the human mind with the broad principles of decency and justice?

1944, 28 AUGUST. (DAWN, 170.)

For Churchill's complete tests of freedom, see Chapter 13.

One must have some respect for democracy, and not use that word too lightly. The last thing which resembles democracy is mob law, with bands of gangsters, armed with deadly weapons, forcing their way into great cities, seizing the police stations and key points of government, endeavouring to introduce a totalitarian regime…

1944, 8 DECEMBER.

...when justice and the law have done their best within their limits, when precedents have been searched and weighed, mercy still roams around the prison seeking for some chink by which she can creep in.

1948, 15 July.

If I was assured that abolishing the death penalty would bring all murders to an end, I would certainly be in favour of that course ... A bargain between politicians in difficulties ought not to be the basis of our criminal law.

Ibid.

Hanging, under English law, if properly conducted, is, I believe, an absolutely painless death.
[Mr. A.E. Stubbs: "Try it."]
Well, it may come to that.

Ibid.

The abuse or misuse for personal gain of the special powers and privileges which attach to office under the State is rightly deemed most culpable, and, quite apart from any question of prosecution under the law, is decisive in respect of Ministers.

1949, 3 February.

It is very much easier and quicker to cut down trees than to grow them. In cases where bad, oppressive laws warp the free development of human society, much cutting down may be needed, and sometimes the forest itself has to be cleared. Great work was done by the Liberal and Conservative Parties in the 19th century, but the 20th century with its terrible events has brought us problems of a different order, not many of which can be solved merely by passing Acts of Parliament.

1952, 6 SEPTEMBER, WOODFORD, ESSEX. (STEMMING, 333.)

The independence of the judiciary from the executive is the prime defence against the tyranny and retrogression of totalitarian government.

1954, 7 APRIL. (ALLIANCE, 137.)

We have history, law, philosophy and literature; we have sentiment and common interest; we have a language which even the Scottish Nationalists will not mind me referring to as English.

1954, 8 AUGUST, ENGLISH-SPEAKING UNION DINNER, LONDON.
(ALLIANCE, 154.)

[King Canute] made a point of submitting himself to the laws whereby he ruled.

1956. (HESP I, 140.)

Canute, now known as Cnut the Great, Viking King of England (1017-35), Denmark (1018-35) and Norway (1028-35).

SIXTEEN

SERVICE

Service, to the state or the people, held Winston Churchill's highest esteem. His admiration was wide: from the miners who 'cut the coal' in the Second World War, the women who manned anti-aircraft batteries, physicians who cured the sick, those in the military services, to the administrators who ran the British Empire.

The scope of this book allows only the bare minimum of Churchill's words praising service to the nation; the reader may consult chapters devoted to the army, navy and air force, and to domestic and international politics, in *Churchill By Himself*. This chapter departs from the usual chronological presentation to list quotations by subtitles for ease of reference.

———

Army
Let me then assure you, soldiers and airmen, that your fellow-countrymen regard your joint work with

admiration and gratitude, and that after the war when a man is asked what he did it will be quite sufficient for him to say, "I marched and fought with the Desert Army." And when history is written and all the facts are known, your feats will gleam and glow and will be a source of song and story long after we who are gathered here have passed away.

1943, 3 FEBRUARY, TRIPOLI. (VICTORY, 10.)

Speech to the Eighth Army.

Britain at war

Service is a sense of justice and a sense of willing association among great bodies of men with the general policy of their country.

1919, 3 MARCH.

As Secretary of State for War, Churchill was organising the orderly demobilisation of the armed forces shortly after the end of the First World War.

There are vast numbers not only in this island but in every land, who will render faithful service in this War, but whose names will never be known, whose deeds will never be recorded. This is a War of the Unknown Warriors…

1940, 14 JULY, BROADCAST, LONDON. (BLOOD, 391-4.)

The whole of the warring nations are engaged, not only soldiers, but the entire population, men, women, and children. The fronts are everywhere. The trenches are dug in the towns and streets. Every village is fortified. Every road is barred. The front line runs through the factories...

1940, 20 August.

"Not in vain" may be the pride of those who have survived and the epitaph of those who fell.

1944, 28 September.

We have our mistakes, our weaknesses and failings, but in the fight which this island race has made, had it not been the toughest of the tough; if the spirit of freedom which burns in the British breast had not been a pure, dazzling, inextinguishable flame, we might not yet have been near the end of this war.

1945, 21 April, Bristol University. (Victory, 116.)

...I should not have been constitutionally debarred from trying to form the strongest Government possible of all who would stand by the country in the hour of peril ... I told [Mr. Attlee] of the authority I had to form a Government, and asked if the Labour Party would join. He said they would. I proposed that they should take rather more than a third of the places, having two seats in the War Cabinet of five, or it might be six, and I asked Mr. Attlee to let me have a list of men so that we could discuss particular offices. I mentioned Mr. Bevin, Mr. Alexander, Mr.

Morrison, and Mr. Dalton as men whose services in high office were immediately required.

1948. (WW2 II, 525-6.)

WSC was writing of the great Second World War coalition government he began to assemble on 10 May 1940.

Coalminers

...some day, when children ask, "What did you do to win this inheritance for us, and to make our name so respected among men?" one will say: "I was a fighter pilot"; another will say: "I was in the Submarine Service"; another: "I marched with the Eighth Army"; a fourth will say: "None of you could have lived without the convoys and the Merchant Seamen"; and you in your turn will say, with equal pride and with equal right: "We cut the coal."

1942, 31 OCTOBER, WESTMINSTER CENTRAL HALL, LONDON.
(END, 261.)

Speech to a conference of mine owners and miners.

Code breakers

[They were] the geese who laid the golden eggs and never cackled.

1940s, PASSIM. (OB VI, 612.)

Colonial service

...look where you will, you will find that the British have ended wars, put a stop to savage customs, opened churches, schools and hospitals, built railways, roads and harbours, and developed the natural resources of the countries so as to mitigate the almost universal, desperate poverty. They have given freely in money and materials and in the services of a devoted band of Civil Servants.

1960. (INGRAMS, VII.)

Commandos

We think of the Commandos, as they came to be called – a Boer word become ever-glorious in the annals of Britain and her Empire – and of their gleaming deeds under every sky and clime. We think of the Airborne Forces and Special Air Service men who hurled themselves unflinching into the void – when we recall all this, we may feel sure that nothing of which we have any knowledge or record has ever been done by mortal men which surpasses the splendour and daring of their feats of arms.

1948, 21 MAY, COMMANDO MEMORIAL DEDICATION,
WESTMINSTER ABBEY. (EUROPE, 337.)

Death in the line of duty

There is something about death on active service which makes it different from common or ordinary death in the normal course of nature. It is accepted without question by the fighting men. Those they leave behind them are also conscious of a light of sacrifice and honour which plays around the grave or the tomb of the warrior...

1942, 8 SEPTEMBER.

H.R.H. Prince George, Duke of Kent, brother of King George VI, was killed in a plane crash in Scotland while on active service with the R.A.F.

Faithful service

Vision, courage, self-denial, faith and faithful service must animate us.

1946, 14 JULY, METZ, FRANCE. (SINEWS, 173.)

Home Guard

...in that terrible summer, when we stood alone, and as the world thought, forlorn, against the all-powerful aggressor with his vast armies and masses of equipment, Mr. Anthony Eden, as Secretary of State for War, called upon the Local Defence Volunteers to rally round the searchlight positions. Shot-guns, sporting rifles, and staves, were all they could find for weapons; it was not until July that we ferried safely across the Atlantic the 1,000,000 rifles and 1,000 field guns, with ammunition proportionable, which were given to us by the Government and people of the United States by an act of precious and timely succour.

1943, 14 MAY, BROADCAST FROM AMERICA. (ONWARDS, 87-8.)

It was Churchill who coined 'Home Guard' as a replacement for the original bureaucratic title, Local Defence Volunteers.

Navy

The warrior heroes of the past may look down, as Nelson's monument looks down upon us now, without any feeling that the island race has lost its daring or that the examples they set in bygone centuries have faded as the generations have succeeded one another. It was not for nothing that Admiral Harwood, as he instantly and at full speed attacked an enemy which might have sunk any one of his ships by a single successful salvo from its far heavier guns, flew Nelson's immortal signal of which neither the new occasion, nor the conduct of all ranks and ratings, nor the final result were found unworthy.

1940, 23 FEBRUARY, GUILDHALL, LONDON. (BLOOD, 270.)

Sir Henry Harwood (1888-1950) commanded the squadron which pursued the German battleship Graf Spee *to Uruguay, where she scuttled herself outside Montevideo, December 1940. Nelson's signal, flown at Trafalgar, was, 'England expects that every man will do his duty'.*

Physicians

There is no profession or calling whose members can feel a greater or deeper conviction of duty of lasting value to be done. There is no profession in which they can feel a surer confidence in an expanding future in their fight against pain and disease.

1947, 10 SEPTEMBER, GUILDHALL, LONDON. (CS VII, 7522.)

Politicians

...service in the House of Commons ranks with the highest service in the State.

1941, 10 DECEMBER. (WW2 III, 755.)

Here in this country, the forerunner of all the democratic and Parliamentary conceptions of modern times, we in this country, who are very old at the game of party politics hard fought out, have learned how to carry through and debate great fiercely-contested political issues without the severance of personal and private friendships.

1944, 9 NOVEMBER.

A friend of mine, an officer, was in Zagreb when the results of the late General Election came in. An old lady said to him, "Poor Mr. Churchill! I suppose now he will be shot." My friend was able to reassure her. He said the sentence might be mitigated to one of the various forms of hard labour which are always open to His Majesty's subjects.

1945, 16 AUGUST.

Royal Air Force

The gratitude of every home in our Island, in our Empire, and indeed throughout the world, except in the abodes of the guilty, goes out to the British airmen who, undaunted by odds, unwearied in their constant challenge and mortal danger, are turning the tide of the world war by their prowess and by their devotion. Never in the field of human conflict was so much owed by so many to so few.

1940, 20 AUGUST

Territorials (Reserves)

When I think how these young men who join the Territorials come forward, almost alone in the population, and take on a liability to serve anywhere in any part of the world … I marvel at their patriotism. It is a marvel, it is also a glory, but a glory we have no right to profit by unless we can secure proper and efficient equipment for them.

1936, 12 NOVEMBER.

Volunteers

A national army is quite different from an army of volunteers, who were produced largely by the pressure in the economic market. I am all for volunteers who come from some uplifting of the human soul, some spirit arising in the human breast.

1947, 6 MAY.

Youth

...Youth, Youth, Youth; efficient youth marching forward from service in the field...

1944, 29 NOVEMBER. (DAWN, 260.)

SEVENTEEN

WAR

Churchill wrote that 'the story of the human race is war', and, at least before the advent of apocalyptic nuclear weapons, regarded wars as recurring phenomena. As a patriot, he urged fighting with 'might and main', which often makes people regard him purely as a warrior, quoting him without context to fit this vision. But no patriot held a more overriding desire for peace, and Churchill strove to avoid both great world wars of the last century.

Once war had begun, his precepts were simple: take the initiative, accept risk, prefer action to inaction, and never surrender. From Queen Victoria's little wars to the Second World War and all the lesser engagements that have followed, many things never change. But in an age where wars are fought but not declared – when declaring war is no longer fashionable – Churchill has much to tell us about the element of chance, the inevitability of mistakes, and the certainty of disappointments before victory is won.

For further quotations refer to the chapters on War, World Wars I and II, and military branches in *Churchill by Himself*.

Advent

Wars come very suddenly. I have lived through a period when one looked forward, as we do now, with anxiety and uncertainty to what would happen in the future. Suddenly something did happen – tremendous, swift, overpowering, irresistible.

1934, 7 FEBRUARY.

Wars do not always wait until all the combatants are ready. Sometimes they come before any are ready, sometimes when one nation thinks itself less unready than another, or when one nation thinks it is likely to become not stronger, but weaker, as time passes.

1936, 10 MARCH.

Balance of forces

If ever a single nation were able to back the strongest fleet with an overwhelming army, the whole world would be in jeopardy, and a catastrophe would swiftly occur.

1912, 18 MARCH.

Great wars come when both sides believe they are more or less equal, when each thinks it has a good chance of victory.

1947, 14 OCTOBER, AL SMITH MEMORIAL SPEECH, LONDON.
(EUROPE, 165.)

WSC delivered his speech to this annual New York fund-raising dinner, which honours the memory of Governor Alfred E. Smith, from London by trans-atlantic telephone.

Blood, Toil, Tears and Sweat

I would say to the House, as I said to those who have joined this Government: "I have nothing to offer but blood, toil, tears, and sweat." We have before us an ordeal of the most grievous kind. We have before us many, many long months of struggle and of suffering. You ask, what is our policy? I will say: It is to wage war, by sea, land and air, with all our might and with all the strength that God can give us: to wage war against a monstrous tyranny, never surpassed in the dark, lamentable catalogue of human crime. That is our policy. You ask, What is our aim? I can answer in one word: Victory–victory at all costs, victory in spite of all terror, victory, however long and hard the road may be; for without victory, there is no survival.

1940, 13 MAY.

First speech as Prime Minister. The famous words had a lengthy gestation. Churchill first deployed 'blood and sweat' in London to Ladysmith via Pretoria *(1900); he used 'their sweat, their tears, their blood' referring to the Russians fighting the Central Powers in World War I in* The Eastern Front *(1931). 'Blood, sweat and tears' came together in his 1939 article, 'Can Franco Restore Unity and Strength to Spain?'* (Daily Telegraph, *reprinted in* Step by Step *('Hope in Spain').*

Commanders

I like commanders on land and sea and in the air to feel they have behind them a strong Government … They will not run risks unless they feel that they need not look over their shoulders or worry about what is happening at home, unless they feel they can concentrate their gaze upon the enemy.

1942, 2 JULY.

You may take the most gallant sailor, the most intrepid airman, or the most audacious soldier, put them at a table together – what do you get? The sum of their fears.

1943, 16 NOVEMBER. (MACMILLAN, 352.)

Conduct

Almost the first of the great principles of war is to seize the initiative, to rivet the attention of the enemy on your action, and to confront him with a series of novel and unexpected situations which leave him no time to pursue a policy of his own.

1917, 21 FEBRUARY.

Let 'em have it. Remember this. Never maltreat the enemy by halves.

1940. 23 SEPTEMBER. (OB VI, 803.)
WSC after giving an order for 100 heavy bombers to attack Berlin.

Costs
War never pays its dividends in cash on the money it costs.

1901, 17 JULY.

All the greatest economists, John Stuart Mill at their head, have always spoken of the evils of borrowing for the purposes of war, and have pointed out that as far as possible posterity should be relieved and the cost of what is consumed in the war be met at the time.

1943, 22 SEPTEMBER.

Diplomatic exchanges
They sound so very cautious and correct, these deadly words. Soft, quiet voices purring, courteous, grave, exactly-measured phrases in large peaceful rooms. But with less warning cannons had opened

fire and nations had been struck down by this same Germany. So now the Admiralty wireless whispers through the ether to the tall masts of ships, and captains pace their decks absorbed in thought. It is nothing. It is less than nothing. It is too foolish, too fantastic to be thought of in the twentieth century. Or is it fire and murder leaping out of the darkness at our throats, torpedoes ripping the bellies of half-awakened ships, a sunrise on a vanished naval supremacy, and an island well-guarded hitherto, at last defenceless? No, it is nothing. No one would do such things. Civilisation has climbed above such perils. The interdependence of nations in trade and traffic, the sense of public law, the Hague Convention, Liberal principles, the Labour Party, high finance, Christian charity, common sense have rendered such nightmares impossible. Are you quite sure? It would be a pity to be wrong. Such a mistake could only be made once – once for all.

1923. (CRISIS I, 48-9.)

End of the Beginning

The Germans have been outmatched and outfought with the very kind of weapons with which they had beaten down so many small peoples, and also large unprepared peoples. They have been beaten by the very technical apparatus on which they counted to gain them the domination of the world. Especially is this true of the air and of the tanks and of the artillery, which has come back into its own on the battlefield. The Germans have received back again that measure of fire and steel which they have so often meted out to others. Now this is not the end. It is not even the beginning of the end. But it is, perhaps, the end of the beginning.

1942, 10 November. Mansion House, London.

Face of war

Ah, horrible war, amazing medley of the glorious and the squalid, the pitiful and the sublime, if modern men of light and leading saw your face closer, simple folk would see it hardly ever.

1900, 22 January. (Ladysmith, 292; Boer, 131.)

The story of the human race is War. Except for brief and precarious interludes there has never been peace in the world; and before history began murderous strife was universal and unending. But the modern developments surely require severe and active attention.

1929. (Crisis IV, 451.)

War, which used to be cruel and magnificent, has now become cruel and squalid.

1930. (MEL, 79.)

…no one can guarantee success in war, but only deserve it.

1949. (WW2 II, 484.)

Length

War is very cruel. It goes on for so long.

1937, 14 APRIL.

Mistakes

…anyone who supposes that there will not be mistakes in war is very foolish. I draw a distinction between mistakes. There is the mistake which comes through daring, what I call a mistake towards the enemy, in which you must always sustain your commanders, by sea, land or air. There are mistakes from the "safety-first" principle, mistakes of turning away from the enemy; and they require a far more acid consideration.

1941, 7 MAY.

War is mainly a catalogue of blunders.

1950. (WW2 III, 316.)

Never Surrender

…we shall not flag or fail. We shall go on to the end, we shall fight in France, we shall fight on the seas and oceans, we shall fight with growing confidence and growing strength in the air, we shall defend our island, whatever the cost may be, we shall fight on the beaches, we shall fight on the landing grounds, we shall fight in the fields and in the streets, we shall fight in the hills; we shall never surrender, and even

148

if, which I do not for a moment believe, this island or a large part of it were subjugated and starving, then our Empire beyond the seas, armed and guarded by the British Fleet, would carry on the struggle, until, in God's good time, the new world, with all its power and might, steps forth to the rescue and the liberation of the old.

1940, 4 JUNE.

Readiness

...if you will not fight for the right when you can easily win without bloodshed; if you will not fight when your victory will be sure and not too costly; you may come to the moment when you will have to fight with all the odds against you and only a precarious chance of survival. There may even be a worse case. You may have to fight when there is no hope of victory, because it is better to perish than live as slaves.

1948. (WW2 I, 272.)

Resistance

One thing is absolutely certain, namely, that victory will never be found by taking the line of least resistance.

1940, 15 JANUARY. (WW2 I, 438.)

It is not only a question of the time that is gained by fighting strongly, even if at a disadvantage, for

important points. There is also this vitally important principle of stubborn resistance to the will of the
enemy.

1941, 10 JUNE.

Responsibility

Any clever person can make plans for winning a war
if he has no responsibility for carrying them out.

1951. (WW2 IV, 499.)

Risk

"Safety first" is the road to ruin in war, even if you
had the safety, which you have not.

1940, 3 NOVEMBER. (WW2 II, 477.)

You have to run risks. There are no certainties in
war. There is a precipice on either side of you – a
precipice of caution and a precipice of over-daring.

1943, 21 SEPTEMBER.

Surrender

Military defeat or miscalculation can be redeemed.
The fortunes of war are fickle and changing. But an
act of shame would deprive us of the respect which
we now enjoy throughout the world, and this would
sap the vitals of our strength.

1941, 27 APRIL, BROADCAST, LONDON. (UNRELENTING, 94.)

Their Finest Hour

What General Weygand called the Battle of France is over. I expect that the battle of Britain is about to begin. Upon this battle depends the survival of Christian civilisation. Upon it depends our own British life, and the long continuity of our institutions and our Empire. The whole fury and might of the enemy must very soon be turned on us. Hitler knows that he will have to break us in this island or lose the war. If we can stand up to him, all Europe may be free and the life of the world may move forward into broad, sunlit uplands. But if we fail, then the whole world, including the United States, including all that we have known and cared for, will sink into the abyss of a new Dark Age made more sinister, and perhaps more protracted, by the lights of perverted science. Let us therefore brace ourselves to our duties, and so bear ourselves that, if the British Empire and its Commonwealth last for a thousand years, men will still say, "This was their finest hour."

1940, 18 JUNE.

Victory

There are two maxims which should always be acted upon in the hour of victory … The first is, Do not be carried away by success into demanding more than is right or prudent. The second is, Do not disband your army until you have got your terms.

1919, 3 MARCH.

I have always urged fighting wars and other contentions with might and main till overwhelming victory, and then offering the hand of friendship to the vanquished. Thus, I have always been against the Pacifists during the quarrel, and against the Jingoes at its close.

1930. (MEL, 346.)

EIGHTEEN
WORK, OPPORTUNITY, INVENTION

If the precepts and theories Churchill expounded under this heading sound antique today, that should be viewed with some sense of alarm by those who still believe in their country. When WSC wrote in the 1930s of 'Mass Effects in Modern Life', he was foreseeing much of which has come to pass under the rubric of government helping people. Beware, Churchill warned, seven and eight decades ago, that you do not shut down opportunity, work and invention by guaranteeing security. Government, in the end, cannot guarantee us against every misfortune, without sapping the spirit of enterprise that throughout history has proven the surest way to prosperity.

Because he believed in popular rule and government by consent, Churchill strove for policies that unite the nation rather than divide it along class lines, as manifested by his powerful arguments on behalf of Free Trade – which in Britain has always been more a political than an economic issue. Tariffs, he feared, would pit the classes against each other by making the staples of life dearer for the people who could least afford them. It may seem inconceivable that this patrician, who loved luxury, could be a warrior for the classless society; yet that is what Churchill was, at a time when it was difficult, for one of his class, to play that role.

Credit and thrift

I was also taught that it was one of the first duties of Government to promote that confidence on which credit and thrift, and especially foreign credit, can alone stand and grow. I was taught to believe that those processes ... would produce a lively and continuous improvement in prosperity. I still hold to those general principles.

1949, 27 OCTOBER.

Enterprise

This is no country of vast spaces and simple forms of mass production ... it is by many thousands of small individual enterprises and activities that the margin by which alone we can maintain ourselves has been procured.

1945, 28 NOVEMBER, FRIENDS HOUSE, LONDON. (SINEWS, 52.)

Among our Socialist opponents there is great confusion. Some of them regard private enterprise as a predatory tiger to be shot. Others look on it as a cow they can milk. [Here WSC made the motion of milking a cow with his hands.] Only a handful see it for what it really is – the strong and willing horse that pulls the whole cart along.

1959, 29 SEPTEMBER, WOODFORD, ESSEX. (ALLIANCE, 324.)
From Churchill's last political speech. Henceforth he was to speak in public only at dedications and memorials, such as at Churchill College and his Woodford Green statue unveiling.

Free Trade
Will the shutting out of foreign goods increase the total amount of wealth in this country? Can foreign nations grow rich at our expense by selling us goods under cost price? Can a people tax themselves into prosperity? Can a man stand in a bucket and lift himself up by the handle?

1904, FREE TRADE HALL, MANCHESTER.
(MACCALLUM SCOTT, 180; PARAPHRASED.)

Industry
…I select four main tests by which to tell what is a depressed industry or an industry which is not flourishing … The first is that unemployment is abnormal; the second, that the ratio of rates to profits is

excessive; the third that the profits are subnormal and the fourth that the profits have been decreasing in recent years.

1928, 5 JUNE.

Inflation and wages

On the whole, when there is inflation and undue expansion, I believe it to be true that wages follow with somewhat slower footsteps the swiftly rising scale of prices.

1925, 4 MAY.

Invention

...the brains, inventiveness, good business management and enterprise of our people enabled our population to double itself in a century. Now here, living, breathing, toiling, suffering, what is to happen if the foundation fails?

1947, 6 DECEMBER, BELLE VUE, MANCHESTER. (EUROPE, 217.)

National Debt

There are two ways in which a gigantic debt may be spread over new decades and future generations. There is the right and healthy way; and there is the wrong and morbid way. The wrong way is to fail to make the utmost provision for amortisation which prudence allows, to aggravate the burden of the debts by fresh borrowings, to live from hand to mouth and from year to year, and to exclaim with Louis XV: 'After me, the deluge!'

1927, 11 APRIL.

Squandermania ... is the policy which used to be stigmatised by the late Mr. Thomas Gibson Bowles as the policy of buying a biscuit early in the morning and walking about all day looking for a dog to give it to.

1929, 15 APRIL.

Opportunity

We are determined that the native genius and spirit of adventure, of risk-taking in peace as in war, shall bear our fortunes forward, finding profitable work and profitable trade for our people, and also we are determined that good and thrifty housekeeping, both national and private, shall sustain our economy.

1945, 15 MARCH, CENTRAL HALL, WESTMINSTER. (VICTORY, 80.)

To release and liberate the vital springs of British energy and inventiveness, to let the honest earnings of the nation fructify in the pockets of the people, to spread well-being and security against accident and misfortune throughout the whole nation, to plan, wherever State planning is imperative, and to guide into fertile and healthy channels the native British genius for comprehension and good will – all these

are open to [the new government], and all these
ought to be open to all of us now … Freedom and
abundance – these must be our aims. The production of new wealth is far more beneficial, and on an
incomparably larger scale, than class and party fights
about the liquidation of old wealth. We must try to
share blessings and not miseries.

1945, 16 AUGUST.

The elimination of the profit motive and of self-
interest as a practical guide in the myriad transactions of daily life will restrict, paralyse and destroy
British ingenuity, thrift, contrivance and good
housekeeping at every stage in our life and production, and will reduce all our industries from a profit-
making to a loss-making process.

1947, 6 DECEMBER, BELLE VUE, MANCHESTER. (EUROPE, 212.)

The commercial and industrial greatness of this
island at the beginning of my lifetime was unri-
valled in the world. All its businesses and firms and
small employers, and careful obliging shopkeepers
were the result of much wisdom and many virtues.
All this was not built up as Socialist speakers would
have you believe by sharks and rogues exploiting
the masses.

1950, 4 FEBRUARY, LEEDS. (BALANCE, 178.)

Perils of the short view

Democratic governments drift along the line of least resistance, taking short views, paying their way with sops and doles, and smoothing their path with pleasant-sounding platitudes. Never was there less continuity or design in their affairs, and yet toward them are coming swiftly changes which will revolutionise for good or ill not only the whole economic structure of the world but the social habits and moral outlook of every family.

1931, DECEMBER, 'FIFTY YEARS HENCE', *STRAND MAGAZINE*.
(THOUGHTS, 202.)

Right to Work

There is not much use in proclaiming a right apart from its enforcement; and when it is enforced there is no need to proclaim it.

1908, 10 OCTOBER, KINNAIRD HALL, DUNDEE. (LIBERALISM, 215.)

Wealth and Redistribution

You may, by the arbitrary and sterile act of Government – for, remember, Governments create nothing and have nothing to give but what they have first taken away – you may put money in the pocket of one set of Englishmen, but it will be money taken from the pockets of another set of Englishmen, and the greater part will be spilled on the way. Every vote given for Protection is a vote to give Governments the right of robbing Peter to pay Paul, and charging the public a handsome commission on the job.

1903, 11 NOVEMBER, BIRMINGHAM TOWN HALL. (FFT, 34.)

The idea that a nation can tax itself into prosperity is one of the crudest delusions which has ever fuddled the human mind.

1948, 21 APRIL, ROYAL ALBERT HALL, LONDON. (EUROPE, 301.)

Socialism is the philosophy of failure, the creed of ignorance, and the gospel of envy.

1948, 28 MAY, PERTH. (EUROPE, 347.)

The choice is between two ways of life: between individual liberty and State domination; between concentration of ownership in the hands of the State and the extension of ownership over the widest number of individuals; between the dead hand of monopoly and the stimulus of competition; between a policy of increasing restraint and a policy of liberating energy and ingenuity; between a policy of levelling down and a policy of opportunity for all to rise upwards from a basic standard.

1949, 23 JULY, WOLVERHAMPTON. (CS VII, 7835.)

BIBLIOGRAPHY

Any quotation annotated only with its date is from the Parliamentary Debates (Hansard), or as transcribed in the *Complete Speeches* (marked CS, see below). All other quotations are identified by page numbers. Works by Churchill himself are conveyed by title words or acronyms, e.g. Crisis for *The World Crisis*, MEL for *My Early Life*. Works by other authors are identified by the author's name and, if he or she wrote more than one work, part of the title, e.g. Gilbert, Life, 89.

Books by Winston S. Churchill

Alliance. *The Unwritten Alliance: Speeches 1953-1959*. London: Cassell, 1961

Balance. *In the Balance: Speeches 1949 & 1950*. London: Cassell, 1951.

Blood. *Blood, Sweat and Tears*. Toronto: McClelland & Stewart, 1941. Published in London as *Into Battle*, 1941.

Boer. *The Boer War*. Combining *London to Ladysmith via Pretoria* and *Ian Hamilton's March*. London: Leo Cooper, 1989.

Covenant. *Arms and the Covenant*. London: George G. Harrap & Co., 1938.

Crisis. *The World Crisis*. 5 vols. in 6 parts. London: Thornton Butterworth, 1923-31.

CS. *Winston S. Churchill: His Complete Speeches 1897-1963*, edited by Sir Robert Rhodes James (8 vols., New York: Bowker, 1974).

Dawn. *The Dawn of Liberation*. London: Cassell, 1945.

End. *The End of the Beginning*. Boston: Little Brown & Co., 1943.

Essays. *Collected Essays of Sir Winston Churchill*. 4 vols. London: Library of Imperial History, 1975.

Europe. *Europe Unite: Speeches 1947 & 1948*. London: Cassell, 1950.

FFT. *For Free Trade*. Sacramento: The Churchilliana Co., 1977. Facsimile edition. First published 1906.

GC. *Great Contemporaries*. Revised and extended edition. London: Leo Cooper, 1990. First published 1937.

Hamilton's. *Ian Hamilton's March*. London: Longmans, Green, 1900.

HESP. *A History of the English-Speaking Peoples*. 4 vols. New York: Dodd, Mead & Co., 1956-58.

India. *India*. Hopkinton, N.H.: Dragonwyck Publishing Inc., 1990. First published 1931.

Ladysmith. *London to Ladysmith via Pretoria*. London: Longmans, Green, 1900.

Liberalism. *Liberalism and the Social Problem*.

Reprinted in *The Collected Works of Sir Winston Churchill*. Vol. VII, *Early Speeches*. London: Library of Imperial History, 1974. First published 1910.

LRC. *Lord Randolph Churchill*. London: Macmillan, 1907. First published in 2 vols., 1906.

MAJ. *My African Journey*. London: Leo Cooper, 1989. First published 1908.

Malakand. *The Story of the Malakand Field Force 1897*. London: Leo Cooper, 1989. First published 1898.

Marlborough. *Marlborough: His Life and Times*. 4 vols. London: Sphere Books, 1967. First published 1933-38.

MBA. *Mr. Brodrick's Army*. Sacramento: The Churchilliana Co., 1977. Reset edition. First published 1903.

MEL. *My Early Life: A Roving Commission*. London: Thornton Butterworth, 1930.

Onwards. Onwards to Victory. London: Cassell, 1944.

People's. *The People's Rights*. London: Jonathan Cape, 1970. First published 1910.

River. *The River War: An Historical Account of the Reconquest of the Soudan*. 2 vols. London: Longmans, Green, 1899.

Sinews. *The Sinews of Peace: Post-War Speeches*. London: Cassell, 1948.

Stemming. *Stemming the Tide: Speeches 1951 & 1952*. London: Cassell, 1953.

Step. *Step by Step 1936-1939*. London: Odhams, 1947. First published 1939.

Thoughts. *Thoughts and Adventures*. London: Leo Cooper, 1990. First published 1932.

Unrelenting. *The Unrelenting Struggle*. Boston: Little Brown & Co., 1942.

Victory. *Victory*. London: Cassell, 1946.

War Corr. *Winston Churchill War Correspondent*, Frederick Woods, ed. London: Brasseys, 1992.

WW2. *The Second World War*. 6 vols. London: Cassell, 1948-54.

WW2 Abridged. *The Second World War*. Abridged 1 vol. edition with an Epilogue on 1945-57. London: Cassell, 1959.

The Official Biography (OB)

Winston S. Churchill, by Randolph S. Churchill (vols. I-II) and Sir Martin Gilbert (vols. III-VIII), together with the accompanying Companion (Document) Volumes was published between 1967 and 1982 by Heinemann, London, and Houghton Mifflin, Boston. Three additional Companion Volumes (*The Churchill War Papers*) were published between 1993 and 2000 by Heinemann and W. W. Norton (New York). In 2006, the complete work began to be reprinted, and seven additional Companion Volumes added by Gilbert, by the Hillsdale College Press, Hillsdale, Michigan. Page references throughout are to the Heinemann editions.

OB I. *Youth 1874-1900.* Published 1966.

OB II. *Young Statesman 1901-1911.* Published 1967.

OB III. *The Challenge of War 1914-1916.* Published 1971.

OB IV. *The Stricken World 1917-1922.* Published 1975.

OB V. *The Prophet of Truth 1922-1929.* Published 1976.

OB VI. *Finest Hour 1939-1941.* Published 1983.

OB VII. *Road to Victory 1941-1945.* Published 1986.

OB VIII. *"Never Despair" 1945-1965.* Published 1988.

OB, CV1/1: *Companion Volume I, Part 1 1874-1896.* Published 1967.

OB, CV1/2: *Companion Volume I, Part 2 1896-1900.* Published 1967.

OB, CV2/1: *Companion Volume II, Part 1 1901-1907.* Published 1969.

OB, CV2/2: *Companion Volume II, Part 2 1907-1911.* Published 1969.

OB, CV2/3: *Companion Volume II, Part 3 1911-1914.* Published 1969.

OB, CV3/1: *Companion Volume III, Part 1: Documents, July 1914-April 1915.* Published 1972.

OB, CV3/2: *Companion Volume III, Part 2: Documents, May 1915-December 1916.* Published 1972.

OB, CV4/1: *Companion Volume IV, Part 1: Documents, January 1917-June1919.* Published 1977.

OB, CV4/2: *Companion Volume IV, Part 2: Documents, July 1919-March 1921.* Published 1977.

OB, CV4/3: *Companion Volume IV, Part 3: Documents, April 1921-November 1922.* Published 1977.

OB, CV5/1: *Companion Volume V, Part 1: Documents, The Exchequer Years 1922-1929.* Published 1979.

OB, CV5/2: *Companion Volume V, Part 2: Documents, The Wilderness Years 1929-1935.* Published 1981.

OB, CV5/3: *Companion Volume V, Part 3: Documents: The Coming of War 1936-1939.* Published 1982.

OB, CV6/1: *The Churchill War Papers, Volume I: At the Admiralty, September 1939-May 1940.* Published 1993.

OB, CV6/2: *The Churchill War Papers, Volume II: Never Surrender, May 1940-December 1940.* Published 1994.

OB, CV6/3: *The Churchill War Papers, Volume III: The Ever-Widening War, 1941.* Published 2000.

Other Works

Boyle, Peter. *The Churchill Eisenhower Correspondence 1953-1955.* Chapel Hill, N.C.: University of North Carolina Press, 1990.

Brook, Sir Norman. 'Diaries of Cabinet Secretary Sir Norman Brook.' New York: *The New York Times,* 22 January 2006; London: *Sunday Telegraph,* 5 August 2007.

Colville, John. *The Churchillians.* London, Weidenfeld and Nicolson, 1981.

Fishman, Jack. *My Darling Clementine.* New York: McKay, 1963.

Gilbert, Martin. *Churchill: A Life.* London: Heinemann, 1991.

Halle, Kay. *Irrepressible Churchill.* Cleveland: World, 1966.

————. *Winston Churchill on America and Britain: A Selection of his Thoughts on Anglo-American Relations.* New York: Walker, 1970.

Hamblin, Grace. 'Chartwell Memories.' *Proceedings of the International Churchill Society, 1987.* Hopkinton, N.H.: International Churchill Society, 1989.

Hyam, Ronald. *Elgin and Churchill at the Colonial Office 1905-1908.* London: Macmillan, 1968.

Ingrams, Harold. *Uganda: A Crisis of Nationhood.* Corona Library. London: HMSO, 1960.

Lysaght, Charles Edward. *Brendan Bracken: A Biography.* London: Allen Lane, 1979.

MacCallum Scott, Andrew. *Winston Churchill.* London, Methuen: 1905.

Macmillan, Harold. *The Blast of War 1939-1945.* London: Macmillan, 1968.

Montague Browne, Sir Anthony. *Long Sunset:*

    Memoirs of Winston Churchill's Last Private Secretary. London: Cassell, 1995.Moran, Charles. *Churchill: Taken from the Diaries of Lord Moran. The Struggle for Survival 1940-1965.* Boston: Houghton Mifflin, 1966.

Nicolson, Nigel, ed. *Harold Nicolson: Diaries and Letters.* 3 vols. London: Collins, 1966-68.

Interviews

Peregrine Spencer Churchill, WSC's nephew; Clark Clifford, aide to President Truman; Ronald Golding, bodyguard 1946-47; Grace Hamblin, secretary 1932-65; Sir John Colville, personal private secretary 1940-55; Sir Fitzroy Maclean, personal representative to Tito, 1943-45; Sir Anthony Montague Browne, personal private secretary 1952-65; Edmund Murray, bodyguard 1950-65; Christian Pol-Roger; Lord and Lady Soames.

INDEX

INDEX

INDEX

INDEX